Letters for My Father:
Grief, Love, and Self-Exploration

Louis Hoffman, PhD

University
PROFESSORS PRESS

Colorado Springs, Colorado
www.universityprofessorspress.com

First Published in 2025, University Professors Press.

Hardcover ISBN:	978-1-955737-65-4
Paperback ISBN:	978-1-955737-66-1
ebook ISBN:	978-1-955737-67-8

University Professors Press
Colorado Springs, CO
www.universityprofessorspress.com

Cover Design by Laura Ross
Cover Image Provided by Lynn Hoffman

Dedication

First and foremost, this book is dedicated to my father, Clarence C. Hoffman, one of the greatest men I have ever known. A man who cared enough to make a difference, caring for and mentoring many people.

To family, who shared our father and husband, Clarence Hoffman: Mom (Lynn Hoffman), John, Joy, Heatherlyn, Mike, Michelle, and Missy.

To my sons, Lakoda, Lukaya, and Lyon, I hope that I can be a good enough father and that the love I received from my father can flow through me to you.

Clarence C. Hoffman

Table of Contents

Acknowledgments

This is different than the books that I have written previously, and it requires a different approach to the acknowledgements, too. First and foremost, I thank my father, Clarence C. Hoffman. This book would not exist if not for his love for me and my love for him. It stands as a testament to it.

When I first considered that these letters might become a book, I knew I needed permission from many people, primarily my family. As I would not publish this book unless it was authentic and honest, I needed their permission to speak to some of the difficulties in my relationship with my father. I started with my mother, then my brother John. Not only did they give me permission, but they gave me encouragement. Next, I needed permission from Mike Sears and Michelle Kuhlmann, my bonus siblings, who, too, offered it. A few friends mentioned in the book also consented to being included.

I also needed permission for letters written to some specific people who were named or discussed. This included my wife, Heatherlyn, and sons, Lakoda, Lukaya, and Lyon. Devlun Whiting also provided permission for the letter written to him. I am grateful to each of these people.

As I share more vulnerably in this book than in any book or article I have written or edited, even the many poetry books, it was important for me to talk through aspects of this vulnerability with close friends. I am thankful for Nathaniel Granger, Jr., L. Xochitl Vallejos, and Shawn Rubin, for being my primary consultants.

Many conversations, some that surprised me, provoked ideas that led to specific letters or aspects of letters. I am thankful for conversations with Lynn Hoffman (mother), John Hoffman (brother), Nathaniel Granger, Jr., Olivia Michael, L. Xochitl Vallejos, Jason Dias, and Jeff Singer that found their way into this book.

The cover for this book was important and symbolic. Thank you to my mother, Lynn Hoffman, for providing the photo. Nathaniel Granger, Jr., and Olivia Michael provided helpful insights in selecting the cover as well.

My brother, John Hoffman, wrote a beautiful epilogue to the book. He managed in four pages to include a beautiful tribute of his own, his own lessons on grieving, and deeply meaningful reflections on the book in an authentic style that matched my writing, once again demonstrating that we are brothers. Olivia Michael and Edbury Enegren were entrusted with early versions of the manuscript and through careful reading extracted lessons on grieving from the book. They endured me sending numerous updates and corrections gracefully. It was difficult for me to find two people who I could trust with the manuscript while I was still struggling with whether it was a good idea to publish this book. They did a marvelous job and demonstrated their worthiness of my trust during a vulnerable time when I was struggling with self-doubt.

Last, I am thankful for the many people who loved my father and helped him be the man and father he became.

Foreword

When I worked in human services, my boss taught me some important stuff about being a man. That mattered at the time. Louis came along later and taught me about being a person.

My dad died badly when I was 19. I didn't know how to handle that. I, the person writing these words at this remove, was barely there. That poor scared kid, alone in a strange world, divorced from his emotions, had no idea what he was feeling, and less idea what to do with those emotions.

Fifteen years later, I got a chance to be in therapy. It was part of therapist training—a mandatory 30 hours. I did that. I had to talk about something, so I talked about my dad. That was useful. But then I met Louis. When I was a graduate student, he had a reputation for being scary. Some viewed him as aloof, arrogant, stand-offish. I listened and stayed away. Then I ended up in his classes because nobody else taught them, and I found out he was quiet, soft-spoken, so you had to lean in to hear what he was saying. And what he was saying was poetry: hard truths and intense emotions filtered through the language of psychology.

He ended up being my clinical supervisor for a couple of terms. That's when I ended up learning how to be a person. It was relevant to a client, so I mentioned my dad. In a couple of observations—"That was a deep breath..."—Louis opened the way for me to step into the human world and feel human things.

When my dad died, I couldn't cry. Didn't know how. Didn't know I should want to. And then, not suddenly but after the culmination of months of work, I was in this room with this man who understood it. I cried, and I wanted to, and it was safe. Now I cry all the time. That's human.

That was another fifteen years ago.

So I spent the morning reading this manuscript, crying off and on, part in empathy because my friend is sharing his pain with us, part in resonance because Keats[1] was right: "beauty is truth and truth beauty."

---

[1] Keats, J. (2019). *Ode on a grecian urn. e-artnow.* (Originally published in 1819)

This is not a feel-good story. It is not a hope-filled narrative about overcoming grief and getting over it, letting go. Nor a simplified, manualized list of steps or stages. Louis hopes somebody will read it and find something in it, but it is not designed to do any work. It is a useless tree: just there, gnarled and alive, being itself. If there is shade to be had, good for us.

Grief is love. You never get over it. Grieving in public is good for something, though. When we lose someone, we keep tripping over their absence. On my dad's birthday, I remember he is not around for me to call. A spouse makes coffee and turns to offer it and is confronted with the absence of their partner. What public grieving seems to do is move the relationship from the external to the internal: from talking out loud and expecting an answer, only to be bereaved again, to talking to the internal working model, that person who is always with us.

This book is that public grieving. A meditation on love, loss, relationships, and regret, in a time when we ignore our shadow at our absolute peril.

I have been pleased to sit with Louis in classrooms, therapy offices, on stages, in virtual places, on planes and trains, buses, and waiting rooms. In each of those places, he is just himself. And now the pleasure of sitting with him in this book, this epistolary call to authenticity, this inner-speech out loud. This is intimacy.

I hope my friend's work is meaningful for him during a difficult time. And perhaps it will be meaningful for you, too.

Jason Dias
May 23, 2025

Introduction for the Reader

My father, Clarence C. Hoffman, died February 28, 2025. Less than a week later, I began writing the letters that would become this book. The letters were first formulated while traveling from Iowa back to our home in Colorado. The ideas were coming so quickly and powerfully that I asked my son to drive beneath the gray and darkening winter sky so that I could begin typing on my iPad. Over the next several hours, the typing flowed continuously. By time we reached Denver, I had 40 pages of letters but had not seriously considered that they might become a book. The writing often came in flurries; the entire first draft of this book was written in just 3 weeks, and the book was compiled with initial editing within 35 days. A few letters emerged during the revisions, but the bulk of this was written during these early weeks of grief. Although I am committed to ongoing self-reflection and processing, this period was the most intense period of self-reflection in many years.

As discussed in Letter 9, "Genuineness and Depth," there has not been a day without tears since my father died, and I anticipate this will continue for many more weeks, if not months. There is peace with this reality. I have become good at grieving and have learned to be deeply happy in the midst of grief and deep sadness. The tears are welcome and will continue to be treasured testimonies of love.

Writing always has been central to my grieving and emotional processing, including journaling, poetry, blogs, tributes, and even scholarly writing. In recent years, it seems I have written too many tributes to those I have lost, including published memorials in journals for two close friends and several briefer memorials on social media. This one is different.

My father grew up on a farm in Leola, South Dakota. He had four older brothers and a younger sister. After high school, he went to South Dakota State, obtained a degree, and became a teacher in Correctionville, Iowa. He was successful as a teacher, including winning an award for his teaching. He began selling insurance during the summer for additional money and eventually purchased a small insurance agency in Charter Oak, Iowa. He grew the insurance agency, which became The Hoffman Agency, into one of the larger insurance agencies in Western Iowa, with 11 different locations and over 50 employees. Later, he ran for the Iowa legislature and served for 10 years in the Iowa House of Representatives. My father became a highly respected person with enormous impact on his local community and the State of Iowa. For his many efforts and accomplishments, he received numerous awards and recognitions.[1]

But this book is not about my father or his accomplishments. This book is about our relationship and my grieving process after he died. Grieving is highly personal. As a psychologist, I have worked with many people struggling with grief. People grieve in different ways. This book is not intended as a manual or to tell people how to grieve. Rather, the purpose is to model aspects of grieving illuminated through my process. I doubt any reader will align with all the approaches to grieving in this book, but I hope everyone who reads it will find some strategies that inspire or resonate with them.

I often have been asked by people the impossible-to-answer question of whether they are grieving correctly. There is no correct way to grieve. While following a structured process of grieving works for some people, many struggle with grieving because they are searching for the "right" way to grieve instead of finding *their* way to grieve. Others encounter obstacles because they avoid topics or aspects of grieving. For example, many encounter barriers due to felt pressure not to say or think anything negative about the deceased or engage with aspects of grieving they view as selfish or self-indulgent (i.e., thinking about their own death or engaging in other self-exploration prompted by grieving).

These letters and the themes addressed in them represent one way to grieve, but this approach—writing letters or writing the type of letters I am writing—would not work for everyone. When my mother dies someday, I imagine my grief will not follow the same path. Different grieving processes may work better for different losses as well. My hope is that readers will find resonance in some of these letters. More centrally, I hope readers will experience liberation to pursue grieving in their own unique and creative ways.

Grieving is sacred process. It mixes sorrow and joy, loss and gratefulness. There are aspects of grieving that I enjoy, and aspects that are devastating. These are intimately connected. In these letters, I strove to face the painful parts directly, with faith that they are connected to

---

[1] My father's full obituary is available at https://www.huebnerfuneralhome.com/obituaries/clarence-hoffman.

the joy even if this could not be seen when the letter began.

This is a book of love, struggle, redemption, self-exploration, forgiveness, and so much more. But most of all, it is a book of love. My life has been blessed with the discovery of many relationships rooted in love. Of these, my love for my father was one of the greatest, and most complicated, of these loving relationships. Even when it hurts, I am always thankful for love, whether it is friendship, romantic, or other types of love. When we open ourselves to any love worthy of the label, we allow our souls to be transformed and expanded through intimate connection and trust of the other person. Real love changes us.

Grieving entails a process of remembering, discovery, and preserving. There is much of my relationship with my father that I do not want to fade away. I want to preserve it and hold on to it with tears and with love. Grieving and these letters have helped accomplish this.

Our Relationship

As is so often the case with familial relationships, my relationship with my father was complex. I loved and admired him dearly. But he was not a perfect father or perfect person. This is not a criticism of him: It is simply the truth. This is the truth of every father, including myself. And I was not a perfect son, either. To grieve for an idealized father would not be authentic; nor could it ever be complete. If we grieve for an idealized person, we do not grieve for a real person. We must grieve for the good and the bad, and for the perfect imperfect.

It is a greater to love someone inclusive of their imperfections than experience a love that only allows one to see the good. It would dishonor my father to write this book in an idealized manner. That is not a book that I can or want to write. In this book, I seek honesty, even though this is not always comfortable.

This is not a book of criticisms or grievances either. The vast majority of the chapters and themes explored are wonderful memories and reflections. For most of my life, I held my father in the highest esteem, even idealized him. While the idealization faded, the admiration and appreciation always remained, even when there was conflict. These letters hold many complexities of our relationship, the closeness and the conflict, the love and the alienation. Many pains from the living years were worked through with these letters, too.

The great gift to myself in this book is that writing it not only preserved the relationship and memories but also drew me closer to my father. As I wrote in these letters, I feel closer to him than I have in many years. These letters have helped me understand him and his limitations better. They helped me forgive him and helped me feel forgiveness from him, too. At times, they helped me forgive myself for not being a perfect son. These were, after all, letters flowing from love, and "Love allows understanding to dawn."[2]

Grieving and Self-Reflection

Death is one of the great illuminators, often compelling us to self-reflection. When others die, it inevitably prompts reflection on our own mortality and aspects of our life. Some people feel guilty engaging in this aspect of grieving and stringently avoid it. However, it is one of the joys and benefits of suffering. I hope that those who grieve me some day will use that opportunity to reflect on their own life. Death is something that unites every one of us. No matter our age, at some point in the future we will return to dust.

As Yalom said, "Though the physicality of death destroys us, the idea of death saves us."[3] One ought not feel guilty for reflecting on one's own life and mortality when a loved one dies. Rather, one can feel existentially blessed by the opportunity to savor the meaning of one's own life while preserving the meaning found in the relationship with their loved one. This process is, after all, deeply connected to love. As bell hooks reflected, "Love empowers us to live fully and die well. Death becomes, then, not an end to life but a part of living."[4]

A portion of this book contains my own self-reflections, some of which may appear tangential. Grief often guides us gently, and sometimes abruptly, to other self-reflection. While, at times, worry emerged that readers may view these as self-indulgent, my intent is to model a powerful, though often neglected, aspect of grieving. The self-reflection examines my father's impact upon me. But it also examines how we were similar and different, which is a part of the person I now am. Through this exploration of myself in contrast to my father, we have become closer. This allowed a discovery and preservation of meaningful aspects of our relationship. After all, he is a significant part of who I have become, for better and worse.

Grieving the death of a parent, spouse, child, or soul friend is different than other forms of grieving. These losses change where we

---

[2] O'Donohue, J. (1998). *Anam cara: A Celtic book of wisdom*, p. 12. Harper Collins.

[3] Yalom, I. D. (1980). *Existential psychotherapy*. Basic Books.

[4] hooks, b. (2001). *All about love: New visions*, p. 197. William Morrow.

are situated in the world, and the world may be experienced as a different place without their presence. My father's death is not the first loss that changed where I was situated in the world. Yet, no prior loss has impacted my situatedness as much. The loss of a parent can thrust us into the community and relationships we have built. It is an opportunity to reflect on and discover if we have chosen wisely. Thankfully, my grief and self-reflection demonstrated to me that I have, for the most part, chosen wisely. These reflections through my grieving have deepened my relational roots with many people whom I love and am coming to love.

Self-reflection opens one to the contingencies of grieving, which I explore often in these letters, particularly Letter 49. The contingencies of grief are connected to the loss and related changes in one's situatedness in the world. These often are not anticipated, or at least aspects of their impact are unforeseen. Many of my relationships were profoundly impacted by my father's death, the shift in my situatedness, and the revelations from the grieving process. Many of these contingencies remain quite raw and painful even as the grief for my father progresses. The contingencies include changes in relationships that have been devastating and others that have been joyous surprises.

Grieving my father opened me to other grieving that I needed to do and did not recognize. This, at times, surprised me as someone who strives to face grief directly. The further grieving was often not about deaths, but other losses, including losses in relationships.

In graduate school, a professor of mine, Winston Gooden, once referred to himself as a "process junkie." I loved that, and it has stayed with me. This deeply resonates, and I could similarly be considered a process junkie. Some of my favorite times in life are spent with friends exploring ourselves and the vicissitudes of life. I am blessed with good friends who enjoy plunging into these depths together; in fact, this seems to be a prerequisite for being a close friend of mine. At times, this is spurred by music, television shows, or movies, but the intersection of art, philosophy, and self-reflection is almost always present. It has never necessitated an advanced degree or having read the existential philosophers; it just requires an openness to exploring the depths of meaning in life, relationships, and ourselves. These days, it is often people who have not read the existential, philosophical, or psychological classics yet have an openness to reflection and inner wisdom that draw my deepest interests.

As I write this, most likely I have already made the bigger decisions of my life: whom to marry, having children, career choice, the friendships in which I root myself. While it is common to say, "I have no regrets," this seems too simple and too cliché. There are regrets, particularly times when I have failed people that I love, including the times when I have not been the son or father I wanted to be. However, the decisions that I have made for meaning, community, and relationships, I do not regret—even the ones that brought pain or broke me. There were good decisions that, often in painful ways, became something else for unforeseen and often unpredictable reasons.

Maybe a life without regrets is not worth living. If one has no regrets, then maybe they have never lived freely. Guilt and regrets are part of who I am. And while there are still ways I hope to grow, I am largely content with the person whom I have become—even when it hurts deeply. Here, I must give myself credit for the community and relationships that I chose and continue choosing as they have shaped the person I am. More than anything, I value my empathy, compassion, commitment to social justice, mutuality, ability to love, proclivity for relational depth, and openness to being broken. These gifts would not live within me without the regrets, guilt, pain, and suffering that I have lived, or without the community and relationships in which I have processed them. If this is the path I had to walk to be blessed with these gifts, I will take it.

While some may view the self-reflection in this book as self-indulgent or even selfish, it is an aspect of the grieving that has blessed me. While some trepidation remains about being publicly vulnerable with some content in these letters, the meaning they have for me—and may have for others—is greater than the hesitation. Maybe, too, if this seems self-indulgent, then this is not the right book for you.

The Process of Writing *Letters for My Father*

Writing has been my most faithful therapist, and one of my best, too. As a therapist, I strongly believe in the value of therapy and that all therapists should return to therapy periodically throughout their life. I have maintained this practice myself. Alongside and between therapists, writing has always been there. There was no question that when my father died, I would be writing: The only question was the form it would take. There is a beauty in the mystery around this. Had I known that my grieving would take the path it did, it would not have been as effective. The mystery and surprises are part of the healing. It was important that I allow for the grieving to take me where I needed to go, whether that be anger, sadness, self-exploration, or the contingencies of grief.

Each letter in this book emerged from a journaling process, not from writing with the intent to publish. The writing process with these letters could aptly be described as verging on *daimon possession*. Existential psychologist Rollo May developed the concept of the daimonic, and defined it as

> any natural function which has the power to take over the whole person. Sex and eros, anger and rage, and the craving for power are examples. The daimonic can be either creative or destructive and is normally both. When this power goes awry and one element usurps control over the total personality, we have "daimon possession..."[5]

During the three weeks when most of the letters were written, I often was consumed by the writing process. At times, an idea, letter, or revision was so powerful and consuming that it became difficult to focus on anything else. As an existential psychologist, I recognized that it was important to listen to this. While often there were seemingly more important things on my to-do list, including impending deadlines, there was an awareness that without giving the grief proper attention it could consume me. The quality of work, too, would have been negatively impacted by forcing myself to prioritize it without giving grief its due.

Many apologies emerged from this daimon possession, as I did not meet some obligations in a timely manner because of being drawn to the writing process. The creativity and meaning that were part of this book converted grief—and its contingencies that had the power to consume me—into something that was freeing, growth facilitating, and beautiful. I am glad that I listened to the beckoning of my grief. Had I not, it is likely that it would have consumed me in more destructive ways.

After the first draft was complete, I began working back through the letters. A few letters were moved to my journal and not included in the book. Others were reshaped, the original versions often kept in my journal. There is appreciation for each letter, whether included in the book or not.

Journaling and letter writing are very personal, and typically private, processes. While I have written or edited 25 books prior to this

---

[5] May, R. (1969). *Love and will*, p. 123. Delta.

one, *Letters for My Father* is the most vulnerable book that I have written. I am a fairly open person. This emerges partially from my values as an existential–humanistic psychotherapist, including valuing vulnerability. Many of the most beautiful experiences of my life were connected to times of vulnerability, such as a story that I share about Jim Bugental in Letter 45, "Coffee with a Friend." Part of my vulnerability is because it is who I am and want to be. During the revision process, after the letters started to form a book, editing allowed me to find the courage to allow my vulnerability to join with an intention to model this aspect of grieving.

As a psychologist, compiling and editing the letters prompted reflections about how I am vulnerable. As discussed in the previous section, part of the grieving process is about self-reflection. As the letters were revised, I strove to maintain their original rawness and honesty while assuring that the letters reflected healthy—or at least healthyish—approaches to grieving.

In the end, this book is a product of facing grieving directly. I wrote this book as a son and as an existential–humanistic psychotherapist who has worked extensively with grieving clients. The topic of the book is myself and my grieving, but the book is not intended to be about me. It is intended to be about grieving. Some people who knew my father may be upset that I spoke to the difficult aspects of our relationship and his imperfections. I can accept their frustrations and anger. However, if I were not to be honest, there would be no reason to allow these letters to become a book. It would not model a healthy or honest grieving process.

When revising these letters for publication, I sometimes thought of clients or students reading these letters. I occasionally felt pulled to censor aspects, thinking about who might read this book. But again, I returned to the realization that if this book was not honest it would be better left to my journals. Modeling an idealized or sanitized grieving process is of no use to anyone.

Furthermore, throughout my entire career I have believed that the person of the therapist is one of the foundations of being a good therapist, and the person of the therapist is human. The "perfect" therapist is less effective at helping people transform their lives than the good enough therapist who is human with their clients. Ruptures, mistakes, and learning on the therapist's part is an aspect of good and effective therapy—and can be the "good stuff" of the therapy process. I was an imperfect son, just as I am an imperfect husband, father, friend, professor, supervisor, and therapist. If I am idealized by some who find their way to this book, sharing my humanness may be shocking. My deepest wish, though, is simply to be good enough—good enough that I may be able to have a positive impact in each of these roles. My life's pursuit is to be good enough that the love, empathy, and compassion that I seek to live by can be felt by those for whom I fill one or more of these roles. If I can do that, then in this life I have been blessed.

I asked several people to read this book in its final stages. My mother, brothers, and sister were asked to read or at least skim the book for aspects related to them or potentially sensitive topics. If they did not want content included, it was important to remove or modify it. I also asked a couple of close friends who know me well to read it and provide feedback on the content.

Primary Symbols

Five primary symbols are followed through this book. These are briefly introduced here. First, the theme of "monsters," draws from James Blunt's song, "Monsters,"[6] which is introduced in the first letter of the book. Second, the symbol of the brown chair, which was a symbol of my father's love for me, re-emerges throughout the book. As symbols hold multiple meanings and can evolve, the brown chair also contains my love for my sons and how this is connected to my father's love for me. Later, it evolves to a symbol of my love for my father as well. The cover of the book with the brown leather background was a suggestion from Nathaniel Granger, Jr., and Olivia Michael, who offered insights that helped select the specific brown leather background used on the book cover. While I could not find a picture of the type of chair that was in my room growing up, this background extends the symbol of the brown chair.

Third, two of my father's most frequent utterances were "I am blessed," and "We are blessed." These seemingly simple phrases encounter great complexity in the book. My father deeply believed he was blessed. Although the phrases were authentic, they also were frequently used in the service of suppression of anything negative. My use of these phrases and a few other variations of this symbol bring more complexity to the idea of being blessed, allowing the symbol to evolve from my father's usage to my own experience of being blessed. My experience of being blessed is different than my father's; one could

---

6 Blunt, Amy W., & Hogarth, J. (2019). Monsters [Recorded by J. Blunt]. On *Once upon a mind* [Album]. Atlantic Records UK.

say it is a more existential understanding of being blessed.

Fourth, the phrase "That's the deal" comes from the movie "Shadowlands." In Letter 4, "I Will Be Grieving You the Rest of My Life," I unpack the meaning of this phrase. In brief, this phrase symbolizes the interconnectedness of the joys of our time together and the sorrow of the ending of that time.

Last, the use of "the living years" is drawn from a song by Mike & the Mechanics titled "The Living Years,"[7] a song that frequented my consciousness for several years approaching my father's death. I strove to say what needed to be said in the living years. However, despite my intentions, there were conversations that never happened. I grieve for these. Some we were not able to have after COVID took some of his cognitive abilities. For some conversations, my courage was lacking until it was too late.

With the death of many close friends in recent years, I have become more focused on telling people how much they mean to me. For example, I have been telling many more people that I love them. Although I am middle-aged and mid-career, hopefully with much life in front of me, it is not too soon for the reality of death to bring vibrancy to the way I live. Indeed, it is never too early to live connected with the vibrancy only death can bring. This is one of the great gifts of grieving and facing death directly. My father's death prompted me to make sure other conversations with people I love are had in the living years. In recent weeks, I have been more honest and vulnerable with some people with whom I am close. While this has, at times, been healing, at other times, it has brought painful wounds, intensifying the grief and even introducing new aspects to it. Even so, there is no regret in these instances of openness. I am willing to embrace the pain necessitated by this honesty and intimacy.

The Organization of This Book

This book is intentionally not written linearly. Grieving rarely follows such an orderly process. Several letters talk about the last days of my father's life. I have spread these out chronologically as the first letter of the first six parts of this book; each of these six letters connects with a different theme in my grieving process explored in that section of the book.

---

[7] Robertson, B. A., & Rutherford, M. (1988). The living years [Recorded by Mike & the Mechanics]. On *Living Years* [Album]. Atlantic, WEA.

There is no end to the grieving process. We must be patient with it, allowing it to take its course. Grieving is not something that we do, but something we live. The journey with grief goes on for our lifetime. Our relationship with it changes and, hopefully, it will not overpower us as much over time. This book has blessed me in reinforcing and deepening my recognition that I can be in the midst of powerful grief and suffering while remaining deeply happy in life. The sadness and grief stand alongside some of the most vibrant aspects of my life and what I treasure most deeply about myself.

Grief is not linear and, at times, becomes circular. Various topics are revisited at different times in the grieving process. There was temptation to reduce the repetition, which I did when the redundancy added no nuances to the story. However, to alter repetition too much would be to distort the grieving process. In grief, we often revisit meaningful parts of our relationship with our loved one. Hopefully, by doing this, there is some change and progress.

In *Our Last Walk: Using Poetry to Grieve and Remember Our Pets,*[8] there is a section on grieving my dog, Amaya. Two of the poems in this section were written about a year apart but shared themes not recognized at first. As I returned to the poems, some subtle shifts in language that emerged became powerful for me. The repetition was not redundancy; it was revisiting. As a psychotherapist, I hear clients tell the same story over and over. Some psychotherapists understandably complain about this. However, I try to listen for how the retold story has changed; in these nuances and differences, great meaning is often held. From these lessons, I chose to mostly retain the repetition to honor the revisiting of potent themes.

Most of the letters in this book are written to my father. However, there are several other letters included. A few letters give voice to my anger; however, when criticisms were made names were withheld, if known. These letters are interspersed in different sections.

Following the letters, there is a chapter written by Olivia Michael and Edbury Enegren on "Lessons from Grieving for My Father." When the letters evolved into a book, their purpose expanded, even if the words written remained the same. Now there was a hope that these letters could be of some benefit to others. At times, it felt audacious to think that my grieving could benefit others. Yet, this is the hope, and without it there is no reason to publish the letters as a book.

---

[8] Hoffman, L. (2016). A visit. In L Hoffman, M. Moats & T. Greening (Eds.). *Our last walk: Using poetry for grieving and remembering our pets.* University Professors Press.

When I began thinking about identifying the lessons in these letters, I encountered strong resistance. While I mention some potential lessons in this Introduction, to compile lessons myself felt inauthentic. Although the letters were informed by wisdom gained from my previous experiences with grieving, reading about grieving, and working with grieving clients, the letters were not written with lessons or modeling grief in mind. It quickly became apparent that if this chapter was included, it could not be written by me.

The final chapter needed fresh eyes. But it was also necessary to be written by individuals who could be trusted with the vulnerability of the content. Olivia and Edbury have been students and supervisees and with whom I have been deeply impressed. In the end, they were two people whom I trusted to have the openness, insight, and wisdom to approach this content in a manner that can illuminate lessons for others.

A Love for Letters

Many years ago, when I first heard the idea of being a "person of letters," I felt a strong affinity with this idea before I even knew its meaning. My association with the phrase was of a reflective scholar who pursues scholarly ideas through letters. This is not far from the traditional meaning, which refers to someone who is an intellectual and often engages in writing and scholarship, particularly related to literature. Today, this phrase resonates within me as the pursuit of intellectual and personal meanings through letter writing in the context of relational depth.

In high school, several important friendships developed through letters. After meeting some people at a convention, I started exchanging letters with them. Later, there were other friendships developed and nurtured through letters. For years, I saved many of the letters sent and received. These friendships built through letter writing often felt deeper and more intimate than friendships carved through time spent together. Later, I began collecting volumes of letters between two people, including the letters between Lu Xun and Xu Guangping,[9]

---

[9] Lu Xun & Guangping, X. (2000). *Letters between two: Correspondence between Lu Xun and Xu Guanping* (B. S. McDougall, Trans.). Foreign Language Press.

Simone de Beauvoir's letters to Sartre,[10] and the letters between Sigmund Freud and Wilhelm Fliess.[11] These fascinated me.

As technology progressed, paper letters were replaced with email. Although I felt a loss with this change, it was easier than handwriting. There were a few close friends, including Mark Yang, Xuefu Wang, and Ed Mendelowitz, among others, with whom I often had deep and meaningful email exchanges, with personal and intellectual themes woven together. These exchanges were treasured, and it has been a source of sadness that now email, too, has become overly burdensome, with the volume of emails often leading to fewer and fewer of these exchanges. There was an intimacy and meaning in letters that has been replaced with a void.

When a letter or email with one of these exchanges arrives, I am excited and eager to read the letter. I can feel the connection of friendship across the miles, whether few or many. However, I generally wait to read the letter or email until I can savor it. Both writing and receiving the letters are potent, and the process brings great joy to my life.

This history with letters surely plays a role in my writing a book of letters for my father. Good letter writing is a hallowed art to me. A song by Dar Williams, "If I Wrote You,"[12] reflects a similar sentimentality with letters. In the song, she is contemplating writing a return letter to someone from whom she was surprised to receive a letter; however, she is worried that this would reveal too much of herself. This could lead to the other person not writing back, and the song hints that hurt or a rupture would come with this. Williams recognizes the power of letters.

The letters in this book often resemble the type of letters I wish I could have exchanged with my father in the living years—letters that embody the spirit of a person of letters. From the context of our relationship, my thoughts often wander to pondering existence itself. I often longed to have the deep philosophical and personal conversations with my father that I pursued and attained in many other relationships. Yet, in letters or conversations such depth eluded us.

If you exchange letters or emails (maybe even text messages) of this type with me, it signifies a trust and an intimacy in the relationship.

---

[10] Beauvoir, S. d. (1992). *Letters to Sartre* (Q. Hoare, Ed. & Trans.). Arcade Publishing.

[11] Freud, S. (1986). *The complete letters of Sigmund Freud to Wilhelm Fliess* 1887–1904 (J. M. Masson, Ed. & Trans.). Belknap Press.

[12] Williams, D. (2019). If I wrote you [Recorded by D. Williams]. On *End of the summer* [Album]. Dar Williams Records.

These letters rarely flow from my pen or keyboard these days, which makes the ones that do even more meaningful. Having such an exchange, most likely means that you are treasured—and loved.

Conclusion: A Letter to the Readers

Dear reader,

I suppose I should thank you for purchasing a copy of this book, but I feel more drawn to thanking you for investing the time in reading it. As I have grown into middle age, choosing a book to read has become rather existential for me. There are many books on my shelf that I will never get to, and others to be written that will draw my desire. As it will not be possible to read all the books that I want to read, choosing a book has become more of an existential choice. I hope this book is worthy of your time.

If you choose to invest in this book, please begin by opening your heart—not to me, or even to my father, but to yourself. The letters were written for me, but they were compiled and published for you. The benefits that I will receive from writing this book have been attained in the writing. Now the book is about you. While this is my story of grief, maybe by exchanging a few details, symbols, and metaphors, you will find yourself in parts of the book, too. My hope is that you use these stories to explore yourself, your relationships, and your losses. Allow your losses to become sacred and treasure them.

You are encouraged to find your pace with this book. The letters are all brief; most are two to three pages. You may choose to read a couple of letters a day or read the book all at once. Like with grieving, it is important to find your pace.

The path of grief is one of the most sacred paths of life. Do not rush through it. Savor it. This is not an encouragement to revel in the pain but rather to explore the beauty with which the pain is so often intimately connected. As you will read in these pages, "That's the deal."

With appreciation,
Louis

Introduction Letter to My Father

Dad,

Before I begin, I need you to know why I allowed these letters originally written to you to become a book. The formulation of this book began the day after your funeral while I was trying to honestly and authentically understand the depths of my grief. I began writing letters to you not knowing that it would become a book. I do not even remember when I started to consider transitioning them in this way.

This is a book of love explored through the grieving process. I loved you very much and am thankful that you were my father. While this book explores the totality of our relationship, including struggles, it is important to me that you, and any readers, know that it is a book of love.

You were an optimist. I long knew this, but in talking with people at the viewing and funeral, it became even more evident that this was one of the most defining aspects of how people viewed you. You always saw the bright side. Even in the minister's sermon at your funeral, the refrain of "I'm blessed" and "We're blessed" were expressed and revisited. Optimism was a blessing for you, and your optimism blessed many people around you.

While you were an optimist, I am an existentialist committed to looking at the world honestly and directly. How an existentialist who revered and often idolized his father emerged from an eternal optimist may seem like a mystery. Yet, as these letters explore, the story makes sense. Through these letters I could see the optimist in you emerge in me more clearly than ever before. This optimism lives very differently in me, but "I am blessed" by its presence.

These letters include good memories and painful ones, with a majority focusing on good memories and reflections. I struggled with including the painful ones because I do not want this to be seen as a book of criticisms and do not want readers to question my love for you. Although you were imperfect, there are few of these imperfections that I hold against you. We were two very different people. We knew many of each other's mistakes and limitations. At times, that created tension and hurt, but it never diminished the love.

As I write this book, the United States is a severely divided and polarized country. This deeply saddened you as it does me. The divides in our country are deeply rooted in political differences and views on race. These were issues we often disagreed about, but we listened to each other and tried to understand. Most important, it never came between our love for each other. I am proud that we were able to keep listening and loving despite these differences, even when the difference included tears, pain, and alienation.

The deepest love is an honest love—a love strong enough to look at the other person seeing all their gifts and flaws, their strengths and imperfections. It is a weak love that can only exist when the other person is idealized. Dad, you deserve the deepest love that I can offer. In these letters I offer you a love that is deeper than I sometimes showed you in life. Hopefully this comes through to anyone who reads these letters.

I loved you very much, Dad. You knew this, just as I knew you loved me. But there were things we never had the chance to finish working through. There were conversations we were never able to complete. For many years I tried, but there was just not enough time. In part, your optimism got in the way. You could only handle these conversations in doses. And I avoided some because your optimism felt like too formidable a barricade to the honesty I sought. In the end, I needed the conversations more than you did, and maybe I did not pursue them hard enough. This my responsibility and a choice that I now live with.

Some of these conversations took over a decade to achieve the progress we made. After COVID, from which your cognitive abilities never recovered, some of the conversations were no longer possible. This is one of the deepest grieving aspects of this book. I wonder if we would have been able to complete these conversations if given another three or four years of you at a place where you were more yourself.

These letters, though written after you were gone, are part of our relationship. They are not dead letters; they are very much alive. The joyous stories and the difficult ones are all written with love. I wish that we could have discussed these in "the living years."[1] Yet, I also recognize that they may be more complete written after your death. I have come to accept that, and these letters deepened that acceptance.

---

[1] Robertson, B. A., & Rutherford, M. (1988). The living years [Recorded by Mike & the Mechanics]. On *Living Years* [Album]. Atlantic, WEA. The song "The Living Years" by Mike & the Mechanics influenced me in the last years of your life and while writing this book.

Through these letters I have come to feel closer to you. That was part of why I wrote them—the longing to feel close to you and preserve the closeness we had. Remembering and preserving meaning is part of the grieving process. These letters preserve much. If no one else reads this book, I am sure to return to it over and over.

If there is some existence after death, and you are able to know of these letters, I hope they provide a testament for how much you meant to me. More than any emotion, I felt love in writing them—even the painful letters. I miss you. I will continue missing you, Dad, for the rest of my days. You have blessed me, and I am grateful that you were my father. Any pain that came with that love was worth it a thousand times over.

With all of my love,
Louis

With my father

Part 1

Chasing Monsters

Letter 1
Chasing the Monsters Away

Dad,

Within the last year, by chance I stumbled across the video of Iam Tongi's American Idol audition,[1] at which he sang James Blunt's song "Monsters."[2] Watching this, I broke down sobbing and have cried, often wept, most times I have watched it since. The chorus of the song talks about chasing the "monsters" away. It is implied that the father, when the son was young, comforted him when scared. Now, as the father is older, it is the son's turn to provide comfort to his aging father—to chase the monsters away. But no description will near the power of Tongi's version of the song.

As you grew older, the monsters would come for you in the evenings. You wanted to be home and could not understand—or remember—why you could not go home. You loved your house, sitting in the sunroom or on the deck, enjoying the view, sleeping in your bed, and just being near Mom. You hated being in confined spaces. Being restricted to a hospital room or nursing home room did not suit you. There was a childlike innocence and purity in aspects of your wanting to be home that were beautiful and endearing, but there were sharper edges as well.

Starting in November, you often became angry in the evenings. The anger was generally directed at Mom. I know you did not mean it, but it could be quite hurtful. This was part of the disease, but I am also convinced this is partially from a life of forced optimism. You did not deal with the negative and were good at repressing it, but as your memory failed so did your defenses and coping mechanisms. All that was repressed began breaking through on those long winter evenings, and Mom was generally the recipient. It really hurt her. When you

---

[1] Iam Tongi's audition on American Idol can be viewed at
https://www.youtube.com/watch?v=S_MAesZsnMk
[2] Blunt, Amy W., & Hogarth, J. (2019). Monsters [Recorded by J. Blunt]. On *Once upon a mind* [Album]. Atlantic Records UK.

recognized her pain, you apologized. Mom knew you did not mean it, too. But it still hurt her.

I downloaded every version of "Monsters" I could find and often watched Tongi's American Idol version, which is my favorite. They became inspiration for my mission to chase your monsters away. John took on the brunt of the assistance. He is better suited to help with the financial matters and the transitions at The Hoffman Agency. Initially, he was also managing the health care. I offered to take over the health care to ease some of John's burden. As a psychologist, I also know the health care side a bit better, too.

Then I volunteered for "monster duty." When you became upset in the evenings, I asked Mom to call or text me, and I then would call you. I also began trying to call as many nights as I could to ward off the monsters before they lashed out at Mom. At first, you expressed your frustration at the situation and anger at Mom. You became convinced in the evenings that Mom did not want you home and this was the reason you were being kept at the nursing home. This was not true, and by the next morning you would know this and were calmer again. It was only in the evenings that the monsters came over you, bringing their anger with them.

Most nights, I convinced you that Mom wanted you home. Through our conversations, I refocused you by talking about things that brightened your mood. Most nights, after we spoke, you did not call Mom. You were better when people were visiting in the evenings. This would last a couple of days before the monsters returned. After a medication change, the evening agitation was less frequent, but you would still try to talk some of us into taking you home or helping you break out.

Some nights you would call while I was teaching a course on existential and humanistic therapy at the University of Denver; it seems so symbolic now. Occasionally, I saw your call but could not answer. Your angst would wander in the back of my mind while I paced through my lectures and conversations, sometimes wondering how your suffering was doing that night. Later, I would call and try to chase some monsters away while driving to supper with Jimmy and Erica, childhood friends from Charter Oak now living in Denver, and you would brighten up asking how they were doing. Monster duty became a sacred honor. It was difficult and very painful, but meaningful. Knowing the agitation and anger were connected to your suffering helped in ways but also led to recognition of the depth of your suffering. Each night, even though I could chase some monsters away, I also felt helpless, unable to rid you of all the monsters and give you what you wanted—to just go home and be in the comforts you worked so hard in your life to bring into existence. If I could bring you some peace, it was worth waging battle with the monsters. The calls brought dread, and most nights they followed a similar trajectory through your ruminations and obsessive thoughts that presented as dark as these winter nights. Alongside the pain, there would be moments of connection and happiness. If I could bring some peace and happiness and ward off the depression and anxiety, I was happy. Now, in a paradoxical way, I treasure those nights.

Love,
Louis

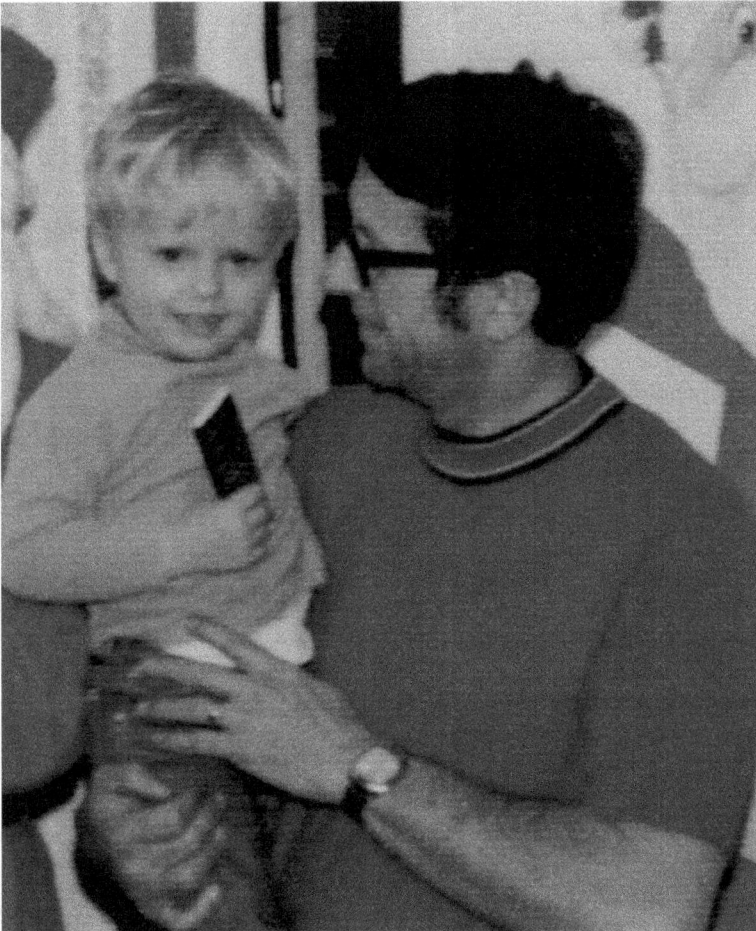

Letter 2
The Brown Chair

Dad,

Over 10 years ago, I wrote a poem for you about my childhood bedroom chair. Through much of early elementary school, I struggled with being scared at night. Some of this was because Mom had been away for periods of time for health issues, and some was because you were often away until late at night. Before John and I had our new bedrooms, I would lay in bed at night not being able to go to sleep until I saw your headlights cross my window, letting me know that you were home. Then sleep no longer resisted.

Nights you were home, I often would cautiously sneak into your bedroom at night, tap your side, and say, "Dad, I'm scared." You would get up, come into my bedroom and sit in the brown desk chair. It was not a comfortable chair with no back support, poor cushioning, and no arm rests. Yet, you would sit there until I went to sleep, no matter how long it took. At the time, I did not think about how uncomfortable you must have been or the consequences of sleep lost; I was just relieved you were there—chasing the monsters away.

After Lakoda was born, he was sometimes afraid at night. He would come and ask me to stay with him. I would lay on the hard floor beside his bed, watching the lights cross the ceiling as cars drove by outside his window. Sometimes, I fell asleep lying beside his bed on the floor. But if I would try to leave before he was asleep, he would get up and beckon me to stay. I would lay back down on that hard floor thinking about how you did the same for me—you stayed.

As I lay in discomfort, the connection with you from many years ago was palpably present. Through that, my connection with Lakoda was also felt. It transformed the experience from something that was annoying and sometimes painful to something to be treasured. I hope I would have stayed with Lakoda even if you had not sat in that brown chair with me, but I do not know. In the end, I am just thankful that in those moments the love from you going through me to my son was present. I am thankful for the thread of love that was sewn and bonded us across generations. Maybe someday Lakoda will feel the connection with both of us as he sits or lays with his own child, passing your love on to another generation.

In 2015, Michael Moats and I were editing a book of poetry on grief and loss, I wanted to include "Brown Chair." It was not a poem of grief— you were still alive. I could not fully explain why I felt it was appropriate and important to include the poem in that book, but Mike allowed it. Likely, I was forcing it. Now I am thankful that it was included.

Brown Chair[1]

for my father

Smooth leather
Buttoned down and
Curved in all the wrong places
That old brown chair
Stayed at my bedroom desk
Rarely used for homework
Or drawing

Yet each night
If the fear came upon me
I would timidly come into your room
And beckon you to allay the fears
You sat patiently
Occupying that lonely brown chair
That was not built for comfort
If you got up before
My eyes stayed closed
I called out
And you stayed

Each night

You stayed

---

[1] "Brown Chair" was written on July 14, 2014 and was originally published in *Capturing Shadows: Poetic Encounters Along the Path of Grieving and Loss*, edited by Louis Hoffman & Michael Moats. (2015, University Professors Press). Republished with permission.

Such a seemingly simple
Act of love
Staying
Being present
Yet not 'til my own young son
Timidly came to my bedside
"Papa"
Did I recognize this sacrifice
This act of love
Frustrated and awakened
I remember being held in your love
And I say
"I'm right here, you are safe now."

And I know
Your love has become
My love

Love,
Louis

Letter 3
Facing Grief Directly

Dad,

The years when I lived in Springfield, Missouri, was a time of grieving. It was also the most joyous period of my life. During this time, I decided that when facing grief, I was going to face it directly and go right into it. Now, this has been my approach much of my life. It is painful, but meaningful.

Facing grief directly helped me move through some of the more difficult aspects of grief more quickly. But this is not the primary reason why I do it. It is because it helps me savor and preserve the meaning of the relationship and lessons learned from it.

When my first marriage ended, this helped me learn about myself, the regrets and mistakes that I made, and move forward more constructively. It also helped me move to a place where I could appreciate the relationship, even if knowing it was not a healthy relationship for either of us. Our paths were going in different directions, and, in retrospect, I take responsibility and the guilt that comes with it for not recognizing our divergent paths before our vows. Grieving restored me to a place where I could care for, even love, the other person.

When moving from a place that I treasured, it helped me preserve meaningful parts of the relationships and community. Springfield was the most salient of these. The three years I lived in Springfield entailed the most rapid and intense personal growth of my life. This, in large part, was due to the amazing friends I developed there. There were friends who cared deeply, supported me, and held me accountable. These friends were interested in and supported my personal and professional growth.

Years later when my dog Amaya died, poetry became my companion, helping me face her death directly. Many poems were written in testimony to my love of Amaya. When returning to these poems over and over, they became even more meaningful to me—even the bad poems. It is part of why *Our Last Walk,*[1] edited with Michael Moats and Tom Greening, was so meaningful to me. Even though you were not a fan of dogs, or really any pets, this was the book of mine that you spoke about most frequently. And I know you gave away many copies of this book to people when their pets died. Seeing your pride was meaningful.

I anticipated that after your death poetry would become my way of engaging the grieving process directly. I was wrong. Turns out I was drawn to letters. This happened naturally and without conscious intent. However, it makes sense. Although I consciously tried to say what needed to be said before you died, there remained much to say. Some of this was things that I could not say because I knew you could not hear them, at least after the cognitive decline and dementia settled in. But there were also things that I did not know I needed to say until I began writing. I learned to appreciate such surprises, even when they were painful. If we listen to what our emotions are telling us, we often find great wisdom in them. It was listening to the emotions that led me to the letters. The letters allowed me to deeply engage the grieving process, for which I am thankful. My love for you needs deep grieving, and these letters have allowed me to do this.

Love,
Louis

---

[1] Hoffman, L. (2016). A visit. In L Hoffman, M. Moats & T. Greening (Eds.), *Our last walk: Using poetry for grieving and remembering our pets.* University Professors Press.

Letter 4
I Will Be Grieving the Rest of My Life

Dad,

After Amaya died, I wrote poems over several years as part of my grieving. Writing and later reading these poems were a cherished part of the grieving process. I still return to these poems. In one of the later ones, "A Visit," the last three lines of a poem were

> And thankfully
> I am still
> Missing you[1]

It is only nine days since you died, but it is evident that this same sentiment will be with me for the rest of my life. I do *not* want to get over losing you. Honestly, that does not even sound tempting. If given the option of a magical pill to no longer feel the pain of grief, it would take less than a second for me to come to my decision—a resounding "no."

Yet, this is not how we are taught to grieve, and even with all my conviction about wanting to hold on to the grief, at times I feel the pressure to conform—to say that I am now okay even if this is not the full truth. As bell hooks wrote,

> grieving individuals are encouraged to let themselves go only in private, in appropriate settings away from the rest of us. Sustained grief is particularly disturbing in a culture that offers a quick fix for any pain. Sometimes it amazes me to know intuitively that the grieving are all around us yet we do not see any overt signs of their anguished spirits. We are taught to feel shame about grief that lingers.[2]

---

[1] Hoffman, L. (2016). A visit. In L Hoffman, M. Moats & T. Greening (Eds.). *Our last walk: Using poetry for grieving and remembering our pets.* University Professors Press.
[2] hooks, b. (2001). *All about love: New visions*, p. 200. William Morrow.

"Shadowlands," which is based in part on C. S. Lewis's book *A Grief Observed*,[3] is one of my favorite movies. The movie draws from Lewis's life, and particularly his relationship with his wife, Joy. After Joy was diagnosed with terminal cancer, Lewis and Joy went on a trip together. As they found respite from the rain on a hike, Lewis tried to avoid a discussion about her dying. In response, Joy states, "The pain now is part of the happiness then. That's the deal."[4] The profundity of this scene always brings tears to my eyes.

But there is more to it. There can be joy in the pain of now. While some tears are just from the pain of loss, they often connect with treasured gifts and memories. I do not enjoy aspects of grieving but am thankful for the grieving process and the gifts that it brings.

As a therapist, I do not believe in giving clients false hope. With grieving, this means that I never tell clients that the grieving process, especially for someone as close as a parent, will end. It changes, but the pattern is different for everyone. I do not know what to expect with my grief path, but it is part of my journey to keep you and the memories of you active in my life.

Still loving and missing you,
Louis

---

[3] Lewis, C. S. (1961). *A grief observed.* Bantam Books.
[4] Attenborough, R. (1993). *Shadowlands* [Film]. Price Entertainment; Spelling Films International.

Part 2

Our Love

Letter 5
A Final Smile

Dad,

On February 26, 2025, I received a text message while I was in session with a client that you had been taken to the emergency room and that conversations about hospice ensued. I did not read the text until after the session was over. During the next three hours, the news evolved quickly. Eventually, I heard from Dr. Luft, your doctor, that we should head home as quickly as possible.

The next 30 minutes were filled with preparations. I called my clients to cancel, contacted my supervisees, arranged coverage at my class and the clinic where I supervise, set up a house sitter for our dogs, told my wife and sons, and packed. We were on the road within a couple hours of the call with Dr. Luft. The first night, Lakoda and I alternated driving until after 2:00 AM, when we were too tired to drive anymore.

We checked into a hotel, and I told my family I wanted to be on the road by 8:00 AM the next morning, emphasizing the importance of leaving on time. Dr. Luft told us that the chemotherapy and antibiotics had been stopped. This meant that your coherence would begin fading. It kept circling in my mind that I had to get there while there was still coherence. We had to be on time. So, we drove on.

There is a clock in my office that was a gift from Jason, a former student and now good friend, that was engraved with a message: "Never on time but always timely." This was preceded by many jokes of my being on "existential time," scheduling arrivals with a time-ish (i.e., 12ish) designation, and recognition of how often I get engrossed in a good conversation, meaningful relationship, or a writing groove, leading me to being late. Maybe some of this is the long Iowa goodbyes that drive Heatherlyn crazy, too. But this trip, I had to be on time. This was a different type of existential time and being late was not an option.

We pushed the driving enough that the next morning I was pulled over for speeding. Not wanting the ticket but even more not wanting to be delayed, I told the police officer who came to the window and asked where I was going that we are going to see my father who was dying.

Tears pushed through my resistance as I completed the sentence and my voice broke, telling of the heartache. Heatherlyn, seeing and feeling my tears, put her hand on my arm. There was worry about whether this was a safe disclosure—words and emotions—with someone whom I had never met in a profession not known for emotional vulnerability. The officer said he would give me a warning—less of a delay, and somehow his compassion meant something, even though it was spoken indirectly in his offer of a warning. This was fitting. You were known for speeding, including getting many speeding tickets and talking your way out of even more.

My worries of being pulled over by the police with my biracial family, something always near my consciousness when driving, was overpowered by my desire to get home. My thoughts remained on getting back on the road, not reminding my sons how to behave or giving them lessons on how to manage the situation if they were to be pulled over, which would have been my usual impulse.

As we neared the hospital, I told my family to drop me off and then head to your house to unpack. I needed to be there as quickly as possible. And I wanted to know what I needed to prepare my sons for when they arrived. When we pulled in, I grabbed my bag and sped to your hospital room. My memories of walking through the hospital that day have a telling vividness—different from the many times I had walked those hallways over the last four months.

When I walked in, a big smile came over your face, and you said, "Louie." I will never forget that smile—that moment. One word, my name, combined with that smile was what I needed for closure. Anything more was a bonus. There was a lifetime of love in that one word and one smile. Oh, Dad, thank you. I needed that.

After that, your coherence faded quickly. Within minutes, words became more difficult. There were few sentences after that moment. Mostly, it was just single words or gestures. But I knew that I arrived in time to feel your love one more time. And maybe it was the deepest I have ever felt it.

Love,
Louis

Letter 6
Papa

Dad,

When my sons were born, Heatherlyn asked me what I wanted them to call me. My answer was "Papa." It is not clear exactly why, but for some reason it felt more intimate. I was aware that Papa is sometimes used for grandfather, and sometimes for Dad. But I was drawn to it. I remember worrying that you might be offended or hurt by my choosing not to be referred to as "Dad," like we referred to you.

From a young child, I longed to be close to you. I wanted to spend time with you and for you to be proud of me. I struggled to know how to ask for closeness, often doing it in ways that I know were frustrating. Though you never intended for me to feel this way, my attempts at spending time with you when I was younger often felt as if I was a burden.

Young children were not your strength. Once adults, Mom shared with us many stories that we later teased you about. For example, you were not good with diapers and only changed a limited amount when John and I were growing up. One time Mom left us with you for a while and John needed a diaper change. You somehow made it through that and then buried the diaper in the snow. After Mom returned, you went back to work. Shortly after you arrived, one of the people from your work called Mom asking if you were okay because you arrived back looking pale and sick.

Mom said you did not know what to do with us until we were old enough to play catch. As we became older yet, it was easier for you and our connection grew. Maybe my draw to the name Papa emerged from a longing for more connection when I was young. While I have not found an answer, the desire for closeness never faded from these early childhood years. You tried, especially when Mom was sick and struggling.

Many memories of childhood are of being alone and not feeling safe when you were not around. You did not know this, and in many ways I am thankful you did not. For years, one of our many babysitters terrified me. There were no incidents of hitting or spanking us, but she yelled and could be mean. She particularly did not like one of my friends, often saying he was a bad influence, yelling at him, too, when he came by.

When you arrived home, I felt safe again. Even as a child, I do not remember blaming you for working so much and being away. I just longed for your presence and, even more, feeling close to you. Still, I long for this.

Love,
Louis

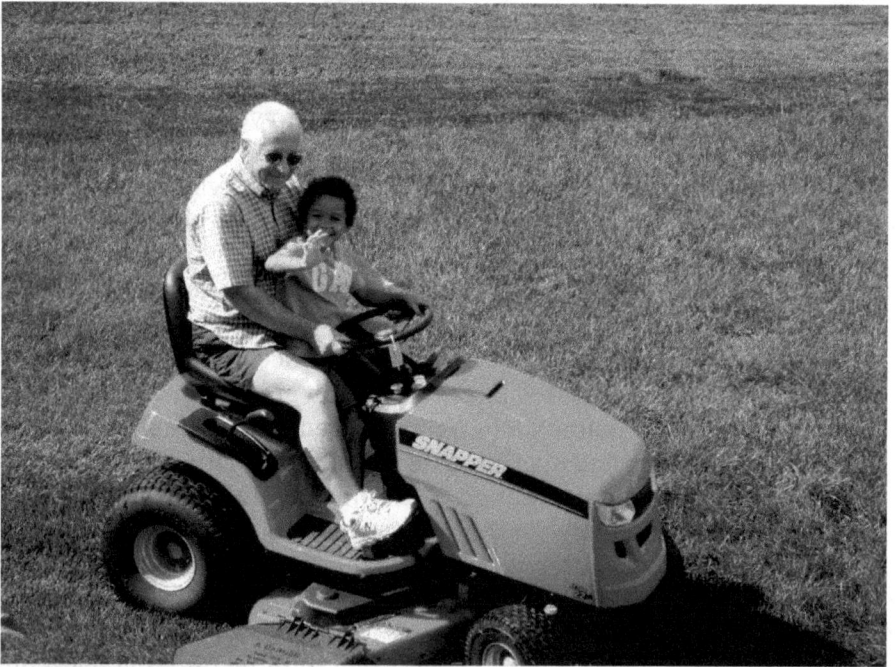
My father with Lakoda, my oldest son

Letter 7
Presence

Dad,

Nathaniel and I led a poetry workshop today, three weeks after you left us. Your presence was strong within me while presenting. Maybe now that you are gone, I will feel your presence more often. I appreciated you being there today. When growing up, you worked a lot and were gone many evenings; however, you never missed a football, basketball, or baseball game. Often, you even recorded these for us to watch afterward. When I watch the copies of these recordings that I converted to digital, I sometimes listen for your voice—your presence.

When I was young, I viewed myself as being lazy. I guess this was, in part, a comparison to you. You worked many hours. During my freshman year, after a broken ankle that was not diagnosed until after my coach also accused me of being lazy, that changed. I started to become a workaholic like you. I was the first one in the gym and stayed as late as I could. My senior year, the nights I did not have high school or town team basketball games, you would often come with me to shoot baskets at the high school gymnasium. I would shoot while you rebounded and threw the ball back. I do not even know how you were able to get a key to the gym to do this, but on many cold winter nights, it was just the two of us in the high school gymnasium shooting hoops. You were present.

For much of your life, you struggled with emotions. When Mom was sick, you knew you needed to fill more of that role so pushed yourself to be there for John and me with our emotional needs. This was not easy for you. While you improved at saying the words, I often did not feel them. As an intuitive person, even from a young age, I needed to feel it. Our communication styles were very different, but I learned to hear your expressions of love in being present, even if it took into adulthood for me to fully recognize and feel this.

Since you died, I have started to become more present to myself again. For three years prior, I had overcommitted to book projects. These were book projects that I felt were important for the field of existential psychology, but they were not what I wanted to be writing, and maybe they helped me hide from other challenges in my life. I wanted to focus on relational depth and social justice issues. These books were a sacrifice. I am proud of them and enjoyed many aspects of the projects, but I found them pulling me more into a "head space." During this time, I did not journal much and rarely wrote poetry. When I did write poems, they were quite poor and often unfinished. I could feel being pulled more to cognitive realms instead of the emotional space that is so important to me.

As the book projects wrapped up, the heart space began returning slowly, but not in all areas of life. Since your death, the emotions have come back more prominently. I feel more myself, more of the person that I want to be. I am still not where I want to be but am getting there. There is some impatience yet, including with my listening, that I want to focus on. Losing you and writing these letters has started a process of reclaiming who I want to be.

When I first began teaching, I talked the school into allowing John and me to teach a graduate psychology class together. A primary focus of the course was exploring different ways of knowing, including art, relationship, and emotion. During one of the classes, there was much sharing and emotion. It was powerful for all of us—students and professors. After the class as John and I were leaving, I turned to him and said, "That is what I want to do with my life." It has always stuck with me and remains true—a symbol of who I want to be and how I want to live. Facilitating deep, emotional connection is something that I love. Those deep connected places are profoundly healing, meaningful, and enlivening. They are also hard to cultivate and maintain. At times, I have failed with these, and at times others have not maintained the shared commitment to these.

This returns me to a place where we were very different. There were just a few times where we attained these deep relational spaces for brief periods of time in our relationship. It happened when I shared that I recognized my first marriage was not going to make it, some conversations about race, and a few times talking about Mom's health, especially when she was very sick and in a coma. But it was rare. I longed for more of that while you were alive. While it never happened as much as I hoped, maybe now we can attain more depth with you gone.

I am still seeking your presence. At times, it feels as if the barriers are gone in both of us. This is not something I believe to be metaphysically true, but symbolically it resonates. Henri Nouwen wrote, "Those you have loved deeply and who have died live on in you, not just as memories but as real presences."[1] The experience of your presence is now alive within me, and I no longer encounter the resistance from you—or from me.

Love,
Louis

Myself, Lyon, and my father

---

[1] Nouwen, H. (1999). *The inner voice of love: A journey through anguish to freedom*, p. 72. Image.

Letter 8
A View

Dad,

Having a view was always important to you. When we lived in Charter Oak, you often spoke of the view we had on top of the hill. You loved it. When you considered moving to Denison (Iowa), you were reticent, I knew, in part because of the view. But you found a place to build that had a view as well. On vacations, you also enjoyed staying in places with a view. At restaurants, you loved dining with a view.

This is something I took from you. Living with a view has also been important to me and an important factor in choosing where to live. Although not always able to afford a place with a view, I have been extremely fortunate to live in many places with stunning views, from the house on stilts in South Pasadena overlooking downtown Los Angeles to our current home with a view of the open space behind our house and the Rockies behind that.

You were proud when I showed you where I lived if there was a view. It may seem small, but it was a meaningful connection. A very fond memory of mine is your visit shortly before you contracted COVID. You never fully recovered from COVID, making this a particularly meaningful visit. Our new deck had recently been finished, and we had an awning installed that allowed us to sit on the deck comfortably even in the hot, bright sun. There are pictures of the two of us sitting on the deck, and some of the two of us with my sons. These are some of my favorite photos of us. In part, it was the bonding over the view. In part, it was the three generations of Hoffmans.

There is a deeper symbolism for both of us in the view. Part of me is drawn to explore it; however, a larger part wants to just appreciate the simplicity of this connection. I do not want to risk ruining it through discovering that we were drawn to having a view for different reasons. Although I generally enjoy seeking the depths even when they seem dark and scary, it feels like there is some wisdom in just letting this one be and observing it.

At this point of my life, I do not have a picture of the afterlife as I did in my youth. Yet, if you still have some form of existence, I hope that you have a view. You earned it.

Love,
Louis

My parents with my sons, and the view from our new deck

Letter 9
Genuineness and Depth

Dad,

You were not one to reveal much about yourself. While you often voiced that you loved me and were proud of me, I struggled to feel it. Our ways of communicating were different. It is not that yours were wrong, but they were different, and we often missed each other.

You were a person of action. It was through deeds that you showed your love. When I was in high school, you showed love through presence at sporting events and going with me to the gym at night to practice my shot. You were my biggest supporter.

After the games, you were always encouraging, including typically telling me, "Good game, Lou." But they were not always good games. When you said this and it did not ring true to me, it caused me to question your praise. One night when I did not play well I became angry and said something after you said "good game." During the other game that week I played well and ended up being named the area Hardees Athlete of the Week. When you showed me, you said something similar to "See, you did have a good game." Your constant optimism and positivity, while it worked for yourself and many others you encouraged, did not work for me. It did not feel genuine, so I resisted it.

When in high school, I sensed this frustration and resistance but did not know what to make of it—a limitation of my youth. I did not have great depth in my relationships at that time. Deep feelings of guilt remain for the women I dated in high school and college. While I was respectful, struggling with the depths must have been painful for them at times. I struggled to say things they needed to hear. Except for my relationship with my brother John, it was not until graduate school that I started understanding what intimacy and depth were about.

During my internship and postdoc in Springfield, my pursuit of the depths intensified. My courage to be vulnerable and open had grown. The intrapersonal depths were also plumbed with assistance from Rollo May, Viktor Frankl, Friedrich Nietzsche, Simone de Beauvoir, and others. During this time, I felt more distant from you. My relationship with my mentor, Robert Murney, was more intimate than my relationship with you. This was a profound time of transition for me. As I was developing deep, meaningful relationships with friends, this stood in contrast to my relationship with you and my romantic relationship. This disparity often felt brutal.

The one time when I felt our connection more deeply was when I was traveling through Des Moines on my way back from a conference. You were in the legislature at this time, living in Des Moines during the week. During the visit, I told you that I thought my marriage was not going to last. Although I was aware you had a marriage before Mom, you had never told me. On this trip, you told me about your divorce, and it was the most intimate, caring support I ever received from you. Without it, I would have remained stuck. Many times, I have longed to relive that day with you in Des Moines—to feel your love and support. The memories are no longer clear, but it seems I can still touch the love I felt that day.

Dad, there is not a day since you died that tears have not cleansed my face. The moment that draws the tears is not always directly connected to you. Many tears have had a joyous presence, such as meaningful interactions with people I care about. Other tears emerged from other relationships where the depths are absent or I have been left feeling alone. Some tears are from looking too honestly at the state of the world, including the lack of compassion in society today or the warnings of possible dystopian times ahead. Often it is a song, or lyric from a song, that comes bursting through. There is a rawness of being that consumes me. Though it may be something else that releases the tears, there is almost always connection with the rawness of losing you. The bandages most effective in soothing tender spaces are cycling in nature and engrossing in the relational depths—places where I can feel deeply myself.

Love,
Louis

Letter 10
Letting You Down

Dad,

When growing up, I never feared punishment from you. After all, you rarely punished us—maybe too rarely. But it did not matter because more powerful than punishment was that I never wanted to let you down. The thought of you being disappointed was much more painful than the thought of punishment. Being grounded or losing privileges I could handle, but feeling your disappointment hurt more deeply than any punishment.

I have never fully been able to explain how this developed, even after years of reflecting on it. Though I felt guilty any time I let you down, it was never shame based. It felt more powerful than shame, and there was no fear of not being accepted or loved. I have wondered about it, journaled about it, and spoken to friends and therapists over the years about this—but even though some pieces have been found, it remains a mystery to me.

There was something beautiful in this desire to never let you down. There was a silent power in it that guided me through much of my life. While it bears similarities with wanting you to be proud of me, there was more to it. It was not about accomplishment. It was about being a good person. While our ideas of being a good person have diverged, part of my desire to be a good person has always been because of you.

I still pursue being a good person, maybe more passionately than anything else in life. It is not a religious conviction. It is not to be admired. It is not out of fear of rejection. It something deeper—something that has become essential to who I have become. Something that feels akin to never wanting to let you down. I am not one to believe in immutable essences, and I do not believe this is just due to having some of your genes. It was something that was developed and nurtured. . . and later chosen. This was not just a cognitive decision; it was a choice embraced with the entirety of my being. As Paul Tillich[1] would say, it

---

[1] Tillich, P. (2001). *The dynamics of faith*. Perennial. (Original work published in 1957)

was an "ultimate concern," something that grips me. To this day, there are still nights where I lay in bed at night struggling with how I can make more of an impact on the world or people who are important to me. Some of these nights are filled with possibilities, others with angst. Occasionally, I wonder if you had nights like these.

Yet, I fail—often. I am too often not the person I want to be. And when I am, I sometimes feel your presence in me. It is not a punishing presence. It is gentle, encouraging. It is one that is up-lifting. It is not only your voice that I hear. Your voice has become part of a chorus of voices—the first one—that I have chosen to internalize. This desire and pursuit of being a good person is also empowered by witnessing countless tears of others—friends, clients, students, and others—that have broken my heart. When I see the suffering of my clients, I know it is, in part, from a broken world. While as a good therapist I can resist the temptation to try to fix them, their tears motivate me to make a positive mark on the world. To not seek this would be to dishonor their tears.

When I became a father, my hope was that my sons would have a similar experience of me, and that they would grow up wanting to be a good person for the right reasons. While Heatherlyn and I are not perfect parents, I think we have done pretty well with this. One time when we met you for dinner in Omaha, Lakoda, then a teenager, saw a person experiencing homelessness outside of the restaurant where we were eating. He went to purchase something for him, and asked if there was more that we could do. I was tearfully proud to see the compassion in him. It was one of his greatest gifts to me.

After you died, my sons showed me a lot of compassion. The evening we left for Iowa, I told them, having to pause for composure, that we had to leave to get back quickly because you would likely die within a couple of days. The pause was not to hide the tears but to wait until I could speak through them. Lukaya was the first to give a hug and then gave me several hugs on the trip home. When I dropped them at my parents' home and prepared to head back to the hospital, Lukaya asked me how I was doing. After I answered, he gave me another hug. Later, Lakoda gave me many hugs. Lyon is a bit young yet, but I could see his concern in his own way, too. In this, I know we did something right.

When I look at my sons and the qualities growing in them, I know some of this is your impact on me that is now impacting my sons. Like the nights in the "brown chair," your love is going through me to my sons, and from my sons to others. As mystifying as it was that the desire to never let you down emerged in me, I am sometimes mystified by how it has developed in them. Though comprehension eludes me, I am thankful.

Appreciatively,
Louis

Family photo from growing up

Letter 11
Music, Touch, and the
Symbols of Love and Grieving

Dad,

Several years ago, I created a playlist called "Father/Son" songs. Some of the songs I associate more with you, others with being a father; most connect with both. I have been listening to this playlist a lot lately—and crying along. I seek the sad songs because they resonate with how I am feeling and because they bring out the emotions to facilitate the grieving process. I have not been one to shy away from grieving—my approach is to face it directly, and sometimes aggressively. This does not work for everyone, but it does for me.

A few songs from this playlist have hit hard. In decreasing order of impact, they include:

- "Monsters," various versions by James Blunt and Iam Tongi, particularly Iam Tongi's version on American Idol[1]
- "Dance with My Father" by Luther Vandross[2]
- "The Living Years" by Mike and the Mechanics[3]
- "Song for My Father" by Jonathon Conant[4]
- "That's My Job" by Conway Twitty[5]
- "Walk Like a Man" by Bruce Springsteen[6]

---

[1] Blunt, Amy W., & Hogarth, J. (2019). Monsters [Recorded by J. Blunt]. On *Once upon a mind* [Album]. Atlantic Records UK.; Iam Tongi's audition on American Idol can be viewed at https://www.youtube.com/watch?v=S_MAesZsnMk

[2] Vandross, L., & Marx, R. (2003). Dance with my father [Recorded by L. Vandross]. On *Dance with my father* [Album]. J Records.

[3] Blunt, Amy W., & Hogarth, J. (2019). Monsters [Recorded by J. Blunt]. On *Once upon a mind* [Album]. Atlantic Records UK.

[4] Conant, J. (2014). Song for my father. [Recorded by J. Conant]. On *Stone cold temple* [Album].

[5] Burr, G. (1987). That's my job [Recorded by C. Twitty]. On *Borderline* [Album]. MCA.

[6] Springsteen, B. (1987). Walk like a man [Recorded by B. Springsteen]. On *Tunnel of love* [Album]. A&M; Kren; The Hit Factory.

As I wrote in another letter, I have been listening to "Monsters" a lot lately. Themes emergent from this song have been common throughout this book. On the rushed drive back to Iowa before you died, I thought of that song often but resisted playing it, in part because I did not want my family to worry about my driving while crying along with that song. The same was true of "Dance with My Father." On Thursday morning, the "The Living Years" came up on my iTunes shuffle. I cried along, but the line really hit me about not being there the day his father died. The tears were set free. Heatherlyn did not notice at first, then gently acknowledged it. Typing these words does as well.

"I have to get home in time," kept reverberating in my head the rest of the drive to the hospital. It was not just getting home before you died but getting home while there was still some of "you" present in your body. It was not until the trip home that I listened to the playlist. Now, I have been listening to it often. I do not resist the pain. I want to go into it. The Father/Son playlist and a Death/Loss playlist I created have kept me feeling. This has kept the grieving process going. It has brought pain and tears as well as deep feelings of joy and connection. I love when these come together.

These also help process aspects of our relationship, and from there prompt journeys into myself. "That's My Job" is a song that fits you well. It tells the story of a father being there for his son in different stages of life and in ways that you have been there for me. From the nighttime child fears to the fears of going "West" to California, much of the song parallels our relationship, with a few symbols and details changed.

"Walk Like a Man," reminds me of how I tried to shape myself after you for much of my life. In the end, thankfully, this was both successful and not successful. We are two very different people. John and Mike share much more similarity with you than I do. I accept this and do not hold any ill feelings about this—anymore. By the time this realization crystalized, I had accepted that we are different people, and I felt good about the direction I chose for my life. Yet, I am always finding more ways that I continue to walk like the man you were. For the ways we are alike, I am generally thankful.

"Song for My Father" is different. The song does not resemble our relationship as closely, at least without exchanging more symbols. But there are two aspects of the song that deeply impact me. First, the line about the day of his father's death, and the shift in emotion, seems to free up tears each time. Second, there is an exploration of the losses of self that are part of the loss of his father—signifying a change in one's situatedness in the world. This is something that has a place in what I have been writing. In ways, these letters have been preserving these parts of myself connected to you. If I can preserve you in me through grief, then grief has a meaning and purpose that transforms the suffering of your loss.

I cannot comprehend, at least not yet, all in me that is lost in your death. About two years before your death, I called you regarding something in the genre of what I frequently sought advice from you about. I recognized the early stages of dementia had taken enough from you that you could not provide the answer being sought. This became more apparent over the next two years. There were times where I felt the pangs of suffering each time this occurred. There was a loss of security with your fading away. I started to search for this elsewhere in my life, but nothing would replace you.

For many, there is a security in one's parents that can never be replaced by anyone else. At first, I did not want to acknowledge this part of the preparatory grief. It felt selfish. I should not be concerned with my security when preparing to face the loss of my father. Over the years leading up to my father death, I could accept these are more natural parts of losing a parent. I still did not like it.

Parents do not just provide security; they symbolize it. This can be seen in songs, poetry, stories, and more throughout history, where the parents' embrace is used to symbolize the deepest comfort. There is another song that I found myself drawn to after my father died that is not even about a father. It is about a child losing their mother: "Mama's Arms" by Joshua Kadison.[7] It is a beautiful and extremely sorrowful song. It was not the literalness but the symbolism that had the impact.

***

Touch plays an important role at the bookends of life. For a baby, touch is part of comfort, co-regulating, and even nurturance. At death, when other forms of comfort lose their power, touch remains. As I write about in other letters, as you approached death, I focused on providing comfort to you through touch. We were not a family of touch. I did not recognize this until marrying a woman from the Bahamas who warned me, on my first visit there, that I would be on touch overload. But in those last days, I knew touch comforted you.

---

[7] Kadison, J. (1993). Mama's arms [Recorded by J. Kadison]. On *Painted desert serenade* [Album]. Hal Leonard Corporation.

Touch is also important during grieving, even built into many rituals connected to the grieving process. At funerals, there are many handshakes, hugs, and other forms of touch. The day of your funeral, John and I surrounded our mother. Rarely was there more than a few minutes at a time when one of us was not providing touch to comfort her.

From the moment Dr. Luft suggested that we come home, I started craving touch. I have shifted from someone who was often uncomfortable with touch the first half my life to greatly appreciating touch—even sometimes craving it. It is one of the ways I feel cared for, and a favorite way for me to express care. Yet, I often feel awkward with it and frequently overthink it, worrying it will be misinterpreted. People often pick up on my awkwardness and, I fear, misread it. It remains difficult for me to initiate touch, even when I desire it or sense the other person desires or needs it, whether it be a handshake, hug, or simple touch on the arm or shoulder. My struggle with this comes from childhood and often has contributed to feeling isolated and alone. While I have worked through much with touch, there is still much work to do.

On the drive back to Iowa, it was my sons, Lukaya, then later Lakoda, often giving me hugs. I could sense their awkwardness and uncomfortableness in offering the hugs, seeing myself in them. I was appreciative of the hugs but felt guilty that my awkwardness with touch was passed on to them. It reminded me of another song, "Arms Wide Open" by Creed.[8] This was a song that I played the day I found out Heatherlyn was pregnant with Lakoda. The lyrics speak to finding out that he will be a father and the hope that his son will be able to face the world with arms wide open. I wanted this for my sons so badly, but the symbolism in their uncomfortableness in offering me the touch I so needed demonstrated my failure. Once again, I cry typing these words.

Touch was not comfortable for you either. I could see this. I do not remember a hug we ever had that violated the "two pat rule" (i.e., you only hug long enough for a quick two pats, then release). When teaching classes and talking about cultural differences, I contrast our family with Heatherlyn's, joking that we could often go a week in our family without touching if we did not accidentally bump into each other in the hallway.

I wonder if you longed for more touch in your life but could not overcome your discomfort to seek it. I wonder if you, too, feared that it would be misinterpreted. I wonder if you repressed your desire for

---

[8] Stapp, S., & Kurzweg, J. (2000). Arms wide open [Recorded by Creed]. On *Human clay* [Album]. Wind-up; Epic.

touch or if you really did not need it. Touch, for good reason, has become controversial in our culture because there has been such a prevalence of unwanted and inappropriate touch. I am now able to recognize how much of a tragedy this is in my own struggle.

Touch, when appropriate, is healing, often beyond what words or any other form of help could offer. Too often we withhold healing by withholding touch. I am certainly guilty of this. Sadly, this is too often necessary. As a therapist, I am cautious about touching my clients, even when I sense that it would be healing. Despite what some risk management workshops, professors, and supervisors often suggest, or even state explicitly, touch in therapy is not necessarily inappropriate. It is critical to use caution given the prevalence of clients who have experienced unwanted or abusive touch, but it can be healing in therapy, too. I feel comfortable writing this, but beyond a handshake it is very rare that I touch my clients. Maybe I could become a better therapist by overcoming this, even if for the occasional hug or more frequent handshakes. Many of my colleagues, especially from different cultures, are more comfortable with appropriate use of touch in psychotherapy.

Many memories are readily recalled of touch that has been profound in my life. Gentle touches on my arm or hand for comfort. Hugs that softened tension or resistance into deep relaxation. Cuddles where the world melted away. Innocent touches that welcomed or invited more relational depth. Touches I will never forget and sometimes can recall viscerally enough to provide comfort that transcends time, such as the touch from your last day.

In your last hours, you were too weak to hug. Yet, I held your hand, touched your arm, and even stroked your face. You never responded with any aversion, and I wondered if maybe you had longed for this all along. There was no doubt in my mind that it offered you comfort.

Maybe this letter wanders too much, but as I look back at it, I do not want to change it. The symbols, in my reading, come together. Your most powerful expressions of love were through symbolism. You often would say to Mom, "Love you, babe" or to your sons, "Love you, Lou" or "Love you, John." These felt as if they were greetings—we had to look beyond the words to see the depth of your love. To a degree, this is always the case. Love, to be authentic, must be lived, not just spoken. Without action, love does not reach its potential and arguably does not really exist. It must be deciphered through the symbols of love. Ideally, living love comes together with words spoken so congruently and powerfully that the love cannot be doubted.

Over the last two years, as several of my friends have died, I have made a commitment to say "I love you" more frequently to people in my life whom I love. This was hard for me to begin doing, and I still cannot overcome my discomfort in some contexts where I feel it would be misunderstood. A few of my friends have responded with surprise, and a couple with discomfort. I have not let it deter me and am cautious to only say it when it is true. I can resonate with their discomfort, having had my own times of awkward pauses and hesitation when friends told me they loved me, especially a couple of female friends. Yet, I appreciate and value their courage to express their love. At a conference shortly after your death, I spoke these words to several friends. The vulnerability of your death played a role in this, but it is also part of a deeper commitment. I have been blessed to have so many people in my life whom I feel love for, and it is important to me that they know. If they are worthy of my love, they deserve my courage to tell them.

Dad, while not always spoken in the ways I wanted to hear them, I know you loved me by the way you lived. That must be enough. Perhaps, it is enough.

Love,
Louis

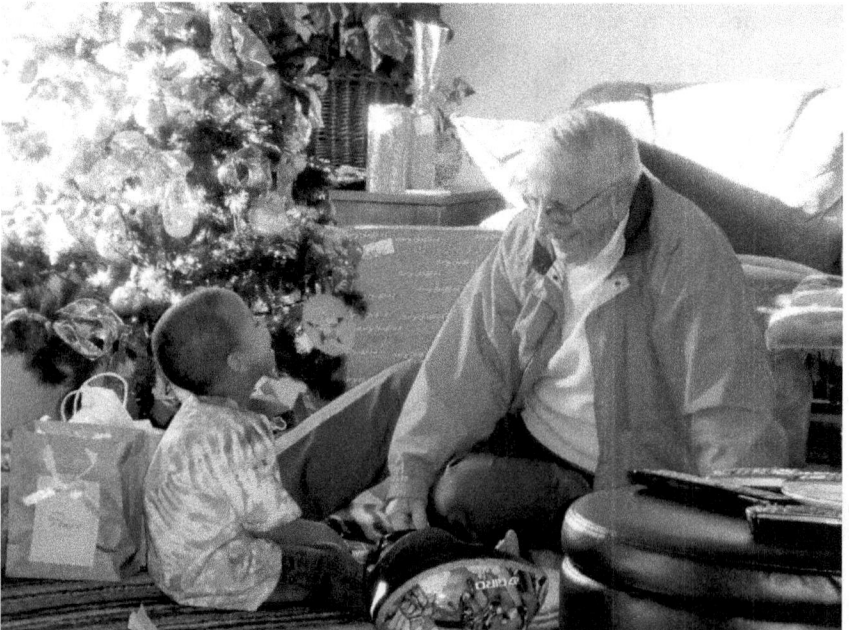

My Father with Lukaya, my middle son

Part 3

Grieving Imperfections

Letter 12
"I Don't Want to be High Maintenance"

Dad,

While I was away for supper the night before you died, you told Mom and the family who was there, "I don't want to be high maintenance." I think this was your second-to-last sentence. You were serious, but it also provided some needed humor. There was comfort in this, too. We had been watching you fade away for a few years, more significantly in the last six months. But these words were very much you. We were saying goodbye to you, not just a fading shadow of you.

You were very independent. This could be frustrating at times. In August 2024, you developed a knee infection. This was the beginning of the slow and painful end. You were hospitalized and never really came home again. There was a brief attempt to bring you home, but it was unsuccessful, resulting in your going to the nursing home. Your dementia was worsening by this time. You could not remember that you were not supposed to walk without assistance. We could never know for sure how much of this was just your stubbornness and independence and how much was not remembering. Surely, it was a combination.

This combination resulted in you falling—a lot. We still marvel that in all these falls you never broke a bone. This, too, is typical of you. You proved everyone wrong with your resilience.

You both loved your independence and hated being a burden. It was difficult to convince you to ask for help. This often resulted in frustrations. We loved you, Dad, and were happy to help. But you did not want help. If you could do it on your own, you would do it—even if you should not.

I have this in me, too. Maybe I should apologize in advance to my sons for what this could mean in 35–40 years from now. For much of my life, I was proud of my independence. After I had three sons of my own, I began to question if this was good for me—and for others. Gradually, I learned to ask for help in some areas some of the time. I am still not great at it, as some of my friends, colleagues, and family will attest. I will still often do things myself to avoid burdening others—even when people urge me not to. But I am better than I was. It is a work in progress.

I am thankful that you taught me to be self-reliant and work hard. But I have also seen the other side of this. At times, not allowing others to help is not allowing people to show their love for you. It is not allowing them to show their appreciation and concern. At times, this feels like a rejection of their love and can create unnecessary worry. I do not know the balance yet—and maybe never will. But this is one more lesson from you that can be preserved through the grieving process.

Love,
Louis

My father

Letter 13
A Good Enough Father

Dad,

In graduate school I came across D. W. Winnicott's idea of the *good enough parent*.[1] I was immediately drawn to it. This was powerful, even though at that time I had not yet allowed for you to become fully human to me. You were still the idealized parent.

My idealization of you was not your fault. It was something that I needed, in part because I had not yet accepted myself as good enough. I still needed something idealized outside of myself that made me okay. You, God, and a girlfriend all seemed to fill those roles at different times. But it was always unfair to the idealized other. My projections were an unfair burden on them.

When John and I were still young, maybe in elementary school or junior high, we each met with Mom's psychiatrist for a one-to-one appointment. When the three of us were sitting in the waiting room, you told John and I that you and Mom were not perfect parents, and it was okay if later we entered our own therapy to work through some of the hurts we experienced from your failures. This was powerful. It is a story that I have told many times to students, parents, and others, including my own sons.

It took years for me to fully understand the power of the gift you gave us in Dr. Brooks' office that day. It was many years before I could acknowledge your imperfections and, with that, your humanity. Yet, as Rollo May discussed, it is often the lessons that we cannot fully comprehend that are the deepest lessons.[2] If we understand them too readily, we check them off and do not think about them. When we must wrestle with the ideas, they become deeper, more personal, and real. This is why I have long preferred the unclear lessons, the ones that do not answer all the questions or quell all the anxieties. These are the best lessons!

---

[1] Winnicott, D. (1973). *The child, the family, and the outside world*. Penguin.
[2] May, R. (1977). *The meaning of anxiety* (Rev. ed). W. W. Norton.

Because you were so idealized, it was devastating when I was forced to reckon with your humanity. I remember clearly the phone call where it happened. It was a while after my divorce. You had been the most compassionate, open, and supportive you had ever been to me during the divorce, especially when I first told you that I thought my marriage was going to end. My idealization of you grew through those conversations.

Much later, after I started dating, came a couple of phone calls that broke my heart, sending me swirling with confusion. The first was when I told you and Mom that there was a Black woman I was interested in dating. A lot had transpired since my divorce. After I knew my marriage was over, I was firmly committed to not entering a serious relationship for a couple of years. I had never just dated people. My relationships went from a first date to a committed relationship. I believed some deep reflection and growth was necessary before beginning a new relationship.

Heatherlyn threw a wrench in that. I was in therapy after my divorce and spent a lot of time trying to eradicate my interest in her. Not because she was Black but because it was not the right time. I spent a lot of time talking with many friends, always trying to talk myself out of my interest in dating her. I explored this in depth with my mentor. To my surprise, as we spoke everyone encouraged me to consider the relationship—friends, family, my therapist, and my mentor.

I worried about telling you that I started dating again but not your reaction to my dating a Black woman. I quickly felt your concerns, but it took me a while to understand them. All I knew was that it hurt, and it challenged my idealizations of you. A few phone calls later, I remember raising my voice at you (something I rarely ever did) and telling you that you needed to enter therapy because you were hurting someone I care about.

What I did not know is that you, too, were ashamed of your reaction and your internalized racism. You did not want this to be a problem, but it was not easy to tell me this. Over time, you gradually did. You shared that one of your concerns was what this meant. You had many friends who made racist comments. Before, you could silently disagree. If your son was dating, and later married to, a Black woman, would you be able to be silent? Would you be able to tolerate their words? Would you feel compelled to address their comments? As someone who hated conflict, these were difficult questions.

Yet, you did your work. It took longer than I wanted and, sadly, you did not live long enough to complete the work, but you faced it and made progress. Mom told me of times when you were with friends who made racist statements that you later addressed with them. You were not one to address this in the group when it was said, but you would, at least at times, say something later in a private conversation.

And I knew you loved Heatherlyn and my sons. You loved them deeply, and you loved Heatherlyn's family. I knew this and know this.

The break in idealization was needed. It allowed for more intimacy and a deeper, more genuine relationship. It created more distance at first, but authentically working through conflict often leads to something better on the other side. It did with us.

I wish I would have allowed you to be human earlier. There were ways you contributed to this idealization, but you were also intentional in that conversation outside Dr. Brooks office to allow for something more. As a parent, I learned from this. I have tried to be open about my humanness and imperfections. Of course, there is a developmental process with this. It is gradual as my children get older. I am sure, too, that I have not done this perfectly. At times, I have revealed too much too soon, and at times I withheld.

This same value has been important to me as a therapist. While idealization is common early in the therapy process and can, at times, be beneficial, I hope that I have become more human to all my clients by time they graduate from therapy. My intent is to offer them a real relationship that is healing. Any real relationship is severely hampered by too much idealization. We are bound together more genuinely through our humanity than through our idealized projections.

Being a perfect father is a heavy burden for children to bear, particularly as they get older. While it is good to be able to admire and appreciate our parents, to do this in the context of perfection is just too much. A good enough parent is better for the child's long term mental health than the perfect parent. In part, this is because the perfect parent is always an illusion. It is far better to have a real parent with whom we can have a genuine relationship.

Dad, you may not recognize all the ways you became human to me over time. You would not be comfortable with some of these. I am sure you would appreciate others. But I am deeply grateful for you preparing the way to allow me to see you as the flawed, but most definitely good enough, father that you were.

Love,
Your hopefully good enough son, Louis

Letter 14
Imperfections, Part 1

Dad,

Fathers are imperfect. I did not fully recognized this until I became a father. I knew it in theory and even taught about this in my courses. I had been drawn to the idea of a "good enough father" and a "good enough mother." But it was when I became an imperfect father that I was thrown into wrestling with the deeper realities of this.

Growing up, I listened to a lot of Bruce Springsteen. I still do. He had a difficult relationship with his father. This was a frequent topic of his songs. Over time, he found redemption in his relationship with his father. One of the times I saw Bruce in concert he talked about being "shocked by your parents' humanity."[1] I was a father by this time, and these words struck me. I bought the concert album after attending and listened to this over and over.

My experience of you was quite different than Bruce's relationship with his father. For me, you were bigger than life. For years I thought of writing a book on lessons I learned from my father. It was not until I was in my 30s that my recognition of your imperfections really took root. You were arguably the most successful person in our little town, at least by the standards of our culture. You were successful in business, financially successful, and admired by many. You also helped many people.

There were several times when friends of mine from high school told me that they had stopped by your office to talk with you. Implicit was always that you really helped them. At first, I was surprised by this, but soon it just made sense.

It was hard to let you be imperfect. You hid many of your imperfections when I was growing up. With it, you hid much of yourself. When you became imperfect, I started to recognize that I did not really know you. And that hurt. Growing up, I often longed for intimacy. I was

---

[1] Bruce Springsteen stated this on March 31, 2016, on "The River Tour" in Denver, Colorado.

lonely as a child and wanted connection. I had friends, but there was not much depth. Even with early girlfriends I hid myself, not knowing how to be more vulnerable. You were perfect to me, and if you remained hidden then it seemed I ought to as well. So, I remained hidden and alone, longing for connection.

This was not your fault. It was what you were taught was a good parent. In ways it worked, but it was hard for a child who longed for intimacy. And more than anything, he wanted intimacy with his father. This is part of my longing for depth as an adult. The ability to cultivate relational depth in professional and personal relationships is something I prize about myself, even though I am very imperfect in its implementation. Yet, there is part of me that wishes I could have discovered this without all the pain. The existentialist in me knows, however, that without the pain it would not have been as authentic of a lesson.

Love,
Louis

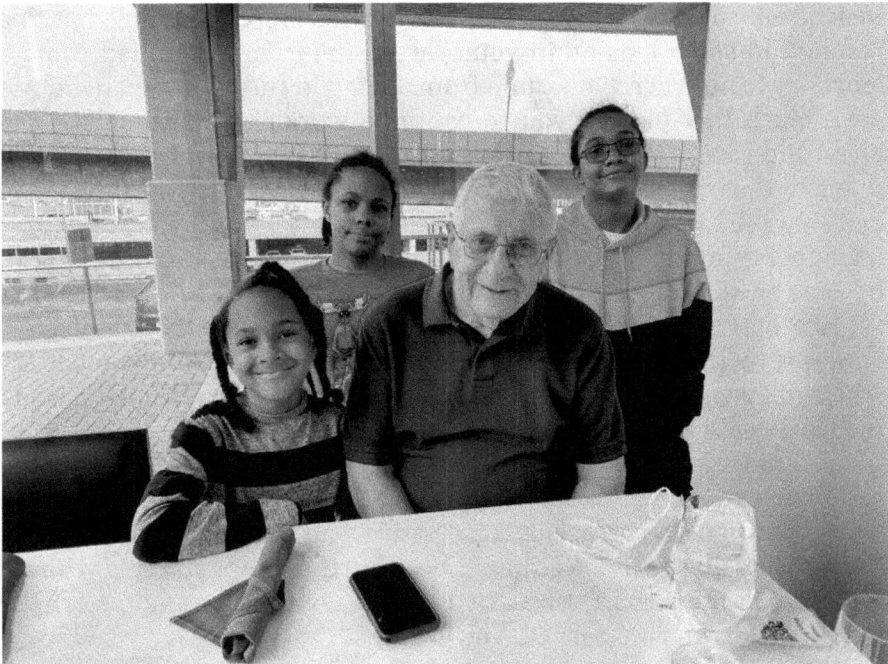

My father on his 90th birthday with my sons

Letter 15
Imperfections, Part 2

Dad,

The biggest challenge to our relationship surely was related to racial issues. I still remember your concern when I first told you that I was dating a Black woman. Without saying anything, I knew your concern—and it hurt. We had more intense conversations around this than any other topic we discussed. The first time you met Heatherlyn, you were silent. This hurt her. I knew, as Mom pointed out, that this was out of your discomfort. Over time, I recognized, too, that you were ashamed of struggling with this.

Rationally, I understood that your mother struggled intensely with racism, which impacted you. Your father was more accepting, but this resulted in some tension in your parents' marriage. You had come a long way from where you came from. Living in rural Iowa, you did not have much that pushed you to continue working on yourself. I also knew the racism around you. One time you told me in a vulnerable moment that part of your struggle was that you felt like you now had to confront the racism every time it was encountered. Now I was not only introducing some difficult conflict, but I was also encouraging you to become an advocate before you were ready.

Heatherlyn appeared more patient than I was, even though she, too, was hurt by this. She told me to be patient. But how could I be patient when you were hurting the woman that I loved. She was right. I pushed too hard, and I know this put a wedge between us.

You did a lot of work, and I am proud of the work you did. I know how much you loved Heatherlyn and the boys. You began to recognize ways that you were racially insensitive and worked to change. On several occasions when we spoke about hurtful things you said without recognizing the impact, I watched as you cried with remorse for the hurt you caused. You learned. You grew.

But as the dementia first started to show itself after COVID, I could see some regression. This, again, hurt. I began to realize that we had reached a time when you were not going to be able to continue to grow and change. Continued growth would be limited by your declining cognitive abilities. This was when I first started grieving. It was a grief that would continue until and beyond your death.

Even after your death, I was reminded of the challenges you faced with this. At your viewing, there were two people who attended who very obviously would not greet Heatherlyn or shake her hand as she stood next to me in the receiving line. After these two couples passed through the line, the rest of the night was impacted. This night should have been an important part of the grieving process, and it was. But it was hampered by the blatant racism of two of your friends.

Living in the midst of such hatefulness had to have been hard for you. I wondered what you would have said had you witnessed this. My guess is that you would not know what to say or do. At most, you might have confronted it privately later. But most likely, you would not have done anything.

As a family, we talked about two people—both politicians—who might attend your funeral that had engaged in some rather blatant racism. If they attended, I had planned to say to them that the best way they could honor you is to leave. My family disagreed because that is not what you would have wanted. It was not who you were. I disagreed, especially if they were attending for political gain. I did not want them to exploit your memory for their gain. But also, I did not want Heatherlyn or my sons to endure racism and hurt because of avoiding a potential conflict.

Looking back on this, I see it is also partially because of my own failures. Not long after I first moved to Colorado Springs, I was asked to attend a meeting with many leaders in the Colorado Springs community. I went with a colleague who knew more people at the event. We were talking to two gentlemen who began discussing the merits of racial profiling. I was furious—and I said nothing. On the drive home, I called and told Heatherlyn. She asked me, "What did they say when you told them you were married to a Black woman?" Immediately, I felt convicted. I had avoided the potential conflict. And I did it because I was representing the school I was working for. I had put business first—*just like you had done.*

I had to learn to take the difficult stands. My nature, a gift from you, is to avoid conflict. But I had to learn as a White man married to a Black woman with biracial children to use my privilege more responsibly. I had to be willing to take difficult stands for my family. I was critical of you for what I was still learning myself, which was unfair. The ethical necessity to explore ourselves in the context of a racist society is never over. And when time ran out for you to learn the lessons I was learning, I had to grieve.

With love and forgiveness,
Louis

Wedding photo

Letter 16
Privilege and Growth

Dad,

A few years ago, I was doing an online workshop while you and Mom were driving to Colorado. Heatherlyn had been working up courage to talk with you and Mom about her experiences as a Black woman in the United States and our family. When you arrived, I was still teaching. That night at supper, Heatherlyn shared her story and experiences. You both listened, cried, and expressed frustration that she had to endure many of these experiences. It was very meaningful for Heatherlyn, and for me as well.

After we had talked through much of this, you said the one thing that really frustrated you was all the talk of White privilege. Heatherlyn smiled and said, "You should ask your son what he was doing today." You looked at me with curiosity and some surprise, and I said, "I was facilitating an all-day workshop on White privilege." There was some laughter and brief awkwardness after my disclosure.

I then shared a story that you had told me several times. It took place early in your insurance career. You were driving home late one night through a small town of less than 500 people. Seeing lights on in a house, you decided to stop and make a sales pitch.[1] The family had insurance. However, after your pitch, the husband said that since you had stopped by at 10:30 at night to make a sales pitch, he knew you would be there if he called at night with an emergency. He switched his insurance to you.

By this time, you had met my friend Nathaniel several times and were fond of him. Nathaniel is a Black man who engages in an incredible amount of service work—and he works hard. After I retold you your story, I said, "Dad, you have always had a good work ethic. You went from poverty to running two very successful businesses that have grown enormously. You absolutely deserve credit for your success. You earned what you have built. But, Dad, if it was my friend Nathaniel who

---

[1] This was long enough ago that door to door sales were still common.

stopped by that house at 10:30 PM at night, how do you think it would have gone?"

You paused, slightly shook your head, and said, "Probably not good." You got it. As we talked more, you were able to understand that privilege is not something to feel guilty for. It does not mean that you had everything given to you or that you have not earned your success. While White privilege sometimes refers to unearned advantage, often it simply means you did not have some of the barriers that others have faced. I was very proud of you for hearing this, taking it in, and understanding.

We had a wonderful weekend after that, including watching the movie "The Hate U Give"[2] with Lyon. You and Mom cried during the movie. I think it was particularly poignant that you had this experience with your youngest grandson. That weekend we sat on our new deck, had great conversations, and enjoyed some amazing sunsets.

At the end of the weekend, you drove home. Within a month, you contracted COVID. Both you and Mom ended up hospitalized from it, but Mom only briefly. Yours was more serious, and you were eventually transferred to Omaha. One day, John called and said they did not think you would survive the weekend. Immediately, I told Heatherlyn and packed. In the middle of packing, I broke down, collapsed on my bed, and sobbed for several minutes. I pulled myself together and was preparing to go when John called back and said there was no reason to come. Because Mom had COVID recently, too, we could not see her. We would not be allowed to see you. It was better to wait—an excruciating wait.

The feelings of helplessness overtook me that weekend. The next day, John said you were doing better. The following day was another good report. You beat the odds. You were in the hospital or rehab for over two months but surprised the doctors and us all. After returning home, you were never the same. The weekend we had shared so recently had been full of such hope and connection. The memories remain as one of my best memories of us together in the last 10 years.

COVID robbed us of the ability to build from that weekend. I am still saddened, even bitter, by what COVID took from us. It is grief of possibilities that could never come to fruition. The weekend provided hope that still lives in me. Hope can still be meaningful even if it is not completed.

---

2 Tillman, G., Jr. (2018). *The hate u give* [Film]. Fox 2000 Pictures; Temple Hill Entertainment.

Love,
Louis

In 2021 at the family farm where my father grew up

Letter 17
Your Insecurities

Dad,

You rarely showed me your insecurities and, when you did, it was partial. I understand why. My impulse is to hide my insecurities from my children and most people in my life except for a few friends. However, as I came to see your insecurities, I longed to know them better. They were a part of you. They helped make you who you are, and I loved them.

In the many conversations I had after you died, people referred to you as humble. That was not the full story. Your humility should not be reduced to insecurities; humility was also a deeply held value of yours. As is typical, the attitudes and behaviors others experienced as humility were empowered by insecurities. Behaviors and the people we become are overdetermined, meaning there are various factors that influence our behaviors and who we are becoming.

You were open to your insecurities with yourself. I do not know how many others you shared them with, but you shared them with Mom, at least at times. The awareness and acceptance of insecurities is important. Though I cannot know because it was not something we discussed, I am confident that you were aware of and, at least to a degree, accepted them. When these are denied or resisted, they often come out in destructive ways. They become what Rollo May referred to as "the daimonic": a natural tendency with the power to take over the whole personality.[1]

You kept your insecurities in check. At times, though, they drove your behavior. You wanted to help others. But most of all, you wanted to make your father proud. You worried that you had failed at that. Much like me, your father was a huge presence in your life. Even after he died, he remained present as an influence. I know that you, too, will remain a presence for me. I welcome that. But I also want to be aware of the various ways that could influence me. They are not all positive.

---

[1] May, R. (1969). *Love and will.* Delta.

You, too, were a generous person. This was a deeply held value and part of who you were as a person. At times, your insecurities pushed you in a way to be more generous than you ought to be. Your generosity hurt you. For example, some people never paid back loans you gave them. Most of these you told me you did not regret. However, some you recognized were bad decisions. I cannot help but wonder if some of those bad decisions were not in the context of your generosity being pushed too far by your insecurities.

From what I have been told, most people do not see my insecurities. Some of these insecurities are rather benign while others are deeply painful to me. Most fall in between. For example, I am quite insecure about my writing. I often hate to read what I have written. When I do and like something I wrote, I am quite surprised. I always assume that I have learned so much since writing previous pieces and imagine what I wrote was worse than reality. It seems I cannot read anything that I have written, even things already published, without the impulse to edit, correct, and improve aspects of the writing. I am sure many would be surprised by this, given that I have written or edited over 25 books. But the anxiety from this insecurity is ever-present. That I have written this much is a testament to the ability I have developed for the joy of writing to stand alongside the constant anxiety, and the courage I have developed to overcome the insecurity when it is time to stop editing and hit send.

My insecurities often are accompanied by loneliness, as I would assume yours were. I have pushed myself to share them more frequently, particularly with students. I want to model to students that the insecurities and anxieties are okay, even if I sometimes think, "Who am I to model this?" Often when I share my insecurities, others are surprised or do not know how to respond. It is often the students' responses that I find the most genuine; even if surprised, they often show appreciation for my sharing them. Many others begin by minimizing them or saying I should not be insecure. That sometimes leaves me feeling more alone.

I wonder how your insecurities played out in your life. Did they live out similar to mine? Did you find an appreciation for them, even when painful? Did you feel alone in your insecurities? Did you find that it was hard to find genuine connection in sharing them?

I longed to know more of your insecurities because I felt that, more than anyone else, connecting with you around insecurities would help me feel less alone in mine. I loved the glimpses of them that I was able to see, but they were few and brief. And I do not think you ever really saw mine, even when I tried to share them. Maybe that was because you were too uncomfortable with your own. I will never know.

But Dad, I want you to know that I loved your insecurities, and I loved you with all of them. I would not want to take them away. I just wanted to sit with them and allow for you to become more comfortable with your insecurities while I become more comfortable with my own.

Love,
Louis

Letter 18
Success

Dad,

We have different ideas of what it means to be successful. Objectively, I believe most people would state that we both have had some success in our careers and life. On the surface, it may even seem that we have been successful in similar ways. However, our pursuits have been very different, and it has led to me often feeling that you did not recognize, or maybe value, my successes. This is not all on you. You have told me how proud you are of me often. You purchased copies of my books, and you have given copies of my poetry books to many people. I know you are proud, but I often did not feel it.

No one who knew you would question that you were highly successful. How could they?! As a teacher, you were popular and even won a Broadcaster Teaching Award. But you quickly transitioned to insurance. Walter Ordway told me a story you shared with him about pursuing a career in insurance. You told him you were deciding between the ministry and insurance, and you decided on insurance because you could provide more practical help and service to people through insurance. This certainly goes against the stereotype of insurance agents.

You were successful in growing the Hoffman Agency from a single small office to a company with 11 locations and over 50 employees. You also built County Risk Management Services and insured over half the counties in the state of Iowa. In these accomplishments, you created financial security and comfort. You were successful in one understanding of the term that fits well with the American Dream and capitalist society.

But you were not a mere capitalist seeking selfish financial gain. There are few that gave more to others than you. You gave to charities, took risks in supporting businesses, and were financially generous. I have often said that if everyone lived like you, trickle-down economics *might* work. Sadly, most people do not, and the result is that trickle-down economics causes much harm while expanding the gap between the wealthy and poor.

We share a commitment to helping others. For me, this is the height of success. Shared tears, laughs, and smiles are a greater measure of success than one's bank account. My career and financial decisions, because of these values, have not set me up for the financial security you wanted. In fact, I still have nights where I struggle sleeping worrying about finances. But it has given me a meaningful life, and that is something I would not trade, even though I often feel some guilt in not being able to do more for my sons and family. I, too, want them to live in a healthy, just world, and my success has been seeking this over personal financial security. By most standards, too, my family is more secure than many.

In businesses I have helped run, I encouraged structures where I am not able to make significant financial decisions, even if in a higher up leadership role. As I told a colleague, "I should not be left in charge of money because I would give it all away." In one private practice I helped run, people working for Heatherlyn and me occasionally made more money than we did. While personally I felt this was the right decision, I never told you about this. It was evident that you would not have approved.

My career decisions have been typically based on meaning over money. This includes taking jobs that paid less and offered less financial security. Some of these you were aware of and did not approve. When I accepted a faculty position at Saybrook University, you told me that this seemed like a good steppingstone. I responded, telling you that Saybrook was my Harvard. For my area of psychology, this was the top school in the world at that time. Sadly, the university changed, and I eventually left because it was no longer the place it was when I began. I left to pursue writing, private practice, and nonprofit work. I was not getting paid for the nonprofit work; any pay was dependent upon benchmarks of success likely to be at least several years down the line. Again, it was a move to less financial security but greater meaning, particularly more service to others.

We both believe in service and helping others. But we have pursued these in different ways. By the values of our society, most would say that you have pursued these in a wiser manner than I have. Maybe they are right.

Our differences often left me feeling unseen by you. What you were proud of was not the accomplishments that gave me the most meaning. I love writing and cannot imagine ever reaching a time when I am not working on at least one book project, even in retirement. Your pride in my books felt good. Yet for me, the deepest meaning was working with students, offering mentorship, helping them launch and succeed in their careers, and helping clients transform their lives. After 19 years in academia, it became evident that I could offer more to students outside of academia. When I was in fulltime academia, the workloads no longer allowed me to give students what I felt they deserved. The values of academia changed to prioritize the quantity of students served over quality of work and relationships with them. Academia left me before I left it. The loss of more meaningful work with students is the primary reason I left.

My academic salary was not great, but it was stable. Financially, I needed to see a day of clients to make ends meet given my academic salary. And I wanted to see clients because the work is meaningful and to sharpen my teaching, supervision, and writing. Academia provided more financial stability than private practice and adjunct teaching. But the stress of the academy while committed to doing quality work was impacting my physical and mental health. Soon after leaving, it felt clear that I made the right decision. My health and happiness improved while working less. You were the primary person I discussed our family finances with, and you were worried about my decision. In ways, I appreciate that you never told me directly that you disapproved.

I wish your approval had not been so important to me—that I could have recognized it as just individual differences and that was okay. But it would not be truthful to say this. After COVID, when your cognitive decline was more evident, I tried to focus on the ways you were proud of me. These could be readily felt and seen, even if not the holistic pride I desired.

Love,
Louis

Letter 19
The Weight of Your Optimism

Dad,

There is a scene from the movie "The Joy Luck Club"[1] that has always resonated with me. A mother and daughter are arguing over the mother's expectations. The daughter is telling her mother that her expectations were too much. The mother responded, clarifying that these were not expectations but hopes for her. The daughter replied, telling her mom that her hopes hurt. I felt this with your hopes, too, but also with your optimism.

Your optimism was revered by many, as we heard over and over at the funeral. But, Dad, your optimism sometimes hurt, too. This optimism was part of why you could never really see me.

In 2016, after Donald Trump was elected, we spoke on the phone as I drove home. Trump made many racist statements during the election and justified or denied much of his history of racism and sexism. These were obvious to anyone honest about what he had said and done. I shared with you my concerns on this day, just a few days after the election. My worries were a bit animated at this moment, in part hoping to wake you from your slumber of not seeing how this could impact your grandchildren. Many of these fears came true during his first term; others are coming true now during his second term.

While we were talking, Mom came into the room and you asked if you could put me on hold, thinking the phone was muted. You did not do this correctly, and I heard you tell Mom that I was just being very negative. When you came back on the phone, I told you that I heard what was said. I remember this feeling of deep calmness that came over me as we spoke, as I explained my fears. You could never hear them, and it hurt.

For you, it was never going to be that bad. Even as you neared death, you would say, "I'm blessed" and "We're blessed." There is a truth in this concurrent with a self-deception. There were so many blessings,

---

[1] Wang, W. (Director). (1993). *The joy luck club* [Film]. Hollywood Pictures. (Based on the book, *The Joy Luck Club*, by Amy Tan.

but you used this to cover over the pain and suffering. They did not go away when you did this; they just remained hidden. Without acknowledging the problem, it is too easy to fall prey to complicity. And too often I felt that you did this. There were only some problems that you could see, but even these you could not see for too long.

This self-deception was part of the distance between us. I am someone who craves genuineness and facing the world and its realities directly. This was too much for you. Sometimes when I needed to be seen and heard, you had to back away, bowing to the protections that optimism and privilege could afford.

Living in a biracial family means some deceptions and complacency are dangerous. Also, being an existential therapist, I learned the power of allowing one's sufferings to be transformed through facing them directly. Rollo May (1982) stated,

> I smile when I note, in conversation with some of my so-called optimistic friends, that when we get down to fundamental issues such as the possibilities of atomic war or the coming food crunch, or the fact that this planet itself will in all probability be wiped out in a finite number of years, their optimism turns out to be a reaction formation to their hopelessness; and I turn out to be more hopeful than they. This is because, it seems to me, one needs a philosophy for oneself that can stand regardless of failure in our actions or temporary despair.[2]

Reading May, I wonder if maybe I was more optimistic than you, or at least authentically optimistic. You feared the dark, forcing the light to enter while typically I am able to sit in the dark, patiently awaiting an authentic, sustainable light to begin to emerge. You could not see me when I was sitting in the dark and did not want to look for me.

You did not fully see, either, what could come from my sitting in the darkness—the most treasured parts of myself. David Elkins, a colleague and friend, wrote,

> If someone told me that I could live my life again free of depression provided I was willing to give up the gifts depression has given me—the depth of awareness, the expanded consciousness, the increased sensitivity, the

---

[2] May, R. (1982). The problem of evil: An open letter to Carl Rogers. *Journal of Humanistic Psychology, 22*(3), 10–21, p. 20.

awareness of limitation, the tenderness of love, the meaning of friendship, the appreciation of life, the joy of a passionate heart—I would say, 'This is a Faustian bargain! Give me my depressions. Let the darkness descend. But do not take away the gifts that depression, with the help of some unseen hand, has dredged up from the deep ocean of my soul and strewn along the shores of my life. I can endure darkness if I must; but I cannot live without these gifts. I cannot live without my soul.[3]

I wonder how you would respond to Dave's words. Would they move you to the depths as they move me? Or would they not resonate through your optimism?

Dad, my grief for you is benefiting others. I see and feel it. There are ways that I am coming more alive as write these letters. I feel more centered in my love for others and do not want to lose this. This is part of why I do not fear journeying into suffering.

Many years ago, a client I was working with had been resisting her emotions more than you often did. One week, I encouraged her to allow herself to be depressed. Her initial facial expression suggested she was wondering what was wrong with her therapist. Nonetheless, she tried. The next week she came in sobbing—and furious at me. Sitting with her that day, I felt this deep, warm connection. I told her that I felt more connected with her that day. She paused, reflected, and commented that she felt more connected with me, too. It was a beautiful moment. She felt her pain and, in allowing herself to feel her depression, she was able to have a deeper, more authentic connection with me. The anger faded away. Something shifted in therapy that day. Our work went deeper and became more effective. This was no magic pill. It was a product of building a therapy relationship, timing, openness, and courage on her part.

Dad, so often I wished for a breakthrough like this in our relationship. There are many weeks and months where I spend more time in deep intimacy with clients than with family. This can be dizzying. Of course, these are one-sided intimate moments contained within the parameters of therapeutic boundaries, but they can be powerful. Not all of them are like the ones I described above, but some are. There is a sadness that I could not, with a few exceptions, have moments like this with you.

---

[3] Elkins, D. N. (1988). *Beyond religion: A personal program for building a spiritual life outside the walls of traditional religion*, p. 188. Quest Books.

Maybe what others benefited from your optimism is more valuable, and has made a greater impact, than would have been achieved by us being able to see each other more deeply. I can live with that. Hearing the stories of how your optimism helped others lessened my pain from not being seen because of it. And for me, I have suffered well with it. The pain has made me a more compassionate, patient, and empathetic therapist and a better person. I get all this and still know that despite the limitations, you loved me.

With forgiveness and understanding,
Louis

My Father with Lakoda, shortly after his birth

Letter 20
The No Handshake

I am not sure who this letter is to. I do not remember your names, and I would not mention them if I did. This is the letter my father would wish that I did not include. I assume some in my family, too, would discourage me from writing it.[1] But for me, it has to be written.

The night of my father's viewing was painful. When I walked into the church and saw his body, I was overcome with emotion. I knew this was going to be a difficult evening. Waiting for people to arrive, the sadness and anxiety was pronounced, only dampened by the distraction of ensuring my sons were okay with their first time seeing a dead body—especially that of their grandfather. It helped that before people arrived, we could sit as a family, watching the slide show with pictures of him, and smile and laugh at memories. I knew there would be people it would be nice to see, and some that would be uncomfortable to see. For many years, it often has been hard to return to Iowa as a biracial family. Even from Facebook, I know that for many we are not welcome, even if it would never be stated outright. We are tolerated—to a degree. At times, we are tolerated because of who I am. At times, we are tolerated because people were too "nice" to speak what they really thought. But often, we are tolerated because of my parents.

Over the years, I heard some of the things said about me marrying a Black woman. Many were cruel and demeaning, made without ever seeking to know anything about Heatherlyn. Sometimes, I just want to scream at people: Heatherlyn is a psychologist who had a 4.0 GPA in her doctoral program. She had one of the highest scores on the licensing exam of anyone that I know. She has published articles, books, chapters, and been a keynote speaker at a national conference. She is an amazing therapist who has helped many people. Former students of hers rave about her as a professor, supervisor, and person. Her impact on the world surely dwarfs those who judge her. On top of all this, years before we met, she was Miss Paradise Island and runner up Miss Bahamas (and

---

[1] I retained the original wording, but I was glad that I was wrong. My family approved of its inclusion in the book.

maybe would have won if not for colorism). But this would not matter. None of this protects her from your judgments and the judgments of so many others.

The comments that I heard were secondhand, so I often did not know how accurate they were. I also heard comments about race that hurt my father and made him uncomfortable. Many years later he told me some of the comments he heard.[2] These hurt. They were part of why I could never return to living in rural Iowa, why I had little interest in class reunions, and why I make little effort to keep up with many people with whom I grew up. I know too much of the racist skeletons hidden in the closets of rural Iowa.

My father, too, had his struggles with me marrying a Black woman, but he had the courage to face them, even if imperfectly. In his latter years, he made some racially insensitive comments that unintentionally caused hurt. When there were conversations about this, he often wept. If he did something that hurt one of his daughters-in-law or grandchildren, this deeply pained him.

He loved his family. I know he loved Heatherlyn and my sons deeply. I know he was pained by friends who continued to say racist things. And I know that he struggled deeply with how to respond. He hated conflict, and one time told me that his greatest fear with me marrying a Black woman was feeling like he would have to start confronting racism when he encountered it. But there were times he rose above his discomfort to confront racism in his calm and gentle way. His calmness, though, did not mean that it did not hurt him.

At the viewing of my father, there were two couples who would not shake my wife's hand. They shook my hand. They shook Michelle and Missy's hand. They shook my mother's hand, and one hugged her. They shook Joy's hand. But they did not shake Heatherlyn's; nor did they acknowledge her existence or humanity even when I introduced her to them. Immediately, I wanted to check with Heatherlyn and make sure she was okay. But there was a line of people that continued flowing past us, so we both said nothing and continued to smile and greet people. Now there was more burden to carry on this already difficult night.

If you could not shake Heatherlyn's hand, then your presence did not honor my father. I know that if he was able to view this, he would have wept seeing Heatherlyn and me hurt by this tasteless act. I know that he would have preferred these individuals never showed their faces.

---

[2] Some of these are too offensive and hurtful to consider including even as examples.

After these couples walked by Heatherlyn, I could not avoid being more on guard. There were other people who I could not tell if they were just socially awkward, introverted, avoidant of eye contact, not wanting to shake anyone's hand, or holding the same sentiments as those who could not acknowledge Heatherlyn's existence. If they, too, were avoiding Heatherlyn because she is a Black woman, it was not as certain as it was with the other two couples. Worrying about this should not have been on my mind at my father's viewing. We buried my father the next day. I should not have had to be on guard about racism or feeling the need to protect my family from it.

In this same church about 10 years earlier, Heatherlyn, our sons, and I went to a Christmas service with my parents, brother, and his family. We arrived around the time the service was starting and the only seats left were the choir seats. These were along the wall toward the front, perpendicular to the other seats. Everyone in the congregation could easily see us, and us them. There was one gentleman who stared at Heatherlyn with what looked like smoldering anger for a brazenly long period of time. I wanted to stand between him and Heatherlyn as a shield or to confront him. How bold to do this in church!

After the service, I asked Heatherlyn if she had noticed. Thankfully, she did not. Her response was, "Maybe he just thought I was beautiful." This was Heatherlyn's way of dealing with it at the time—a psychological defense—and I appreciated that. It is hard to be Black in rural Iowa, and some defenses were necessary. But I know it hurt, and over the years events such as this have built up for both of us. Yet my pain was not the same as hers. My skin protects me from fully understanding her pain and experience. The inevitableness of this type of separation in a society rooted in racism is excruciating at times. When driving across Nebraska and rural Iowa, I am almost always on guard—ready to protect my family. It is not protecting them necessarily from physical violence, but the psychological pain embedded in the looks, jeers, and other behaviors—such as that of one woman during Heatherlyn's and my first time driving in rural Nebraska together. When Heatherlyn entered a gas station, the woman grabbed her husband's arm, pulled him close, and asked in a panic if he had locked their car. That reinforced to me that driving across rural Nebraska and Iowa would never again be the same experience.

During COVID, we took a family vacation to the Black Hills of South Dakota and then to Minnesota. On the trip, the frequency of racism we encountered was the most Heatherlyn and I had ever experienced. We later joked about this being our family racism tour. This trip was also when one of my sons first became socially aware of racism, to the point where he did not want to eat in restaurants on the trip. The weight of the stares, gazes, and reactions to our presence became too much. It seemed at each stop we encountered something ranging from microaggression to telling stares that could not have been any clearer if stated in racial slurs. At one town in South Dakota where we were planning to stay, Heatherlyn and my son were so uncomfortable with the looks we received that we gave up our reservation to drive further to a larger city where, hopefully, we could escape the gazes.

On this trip, we met my parents in the town where my father grew up. Again, racism could not be avoided. We were suspiciously confronted when taking a picture at the town sign. Shortly after this, we went into the local grocery store. I walked in first and was given a greeting. When my son and Heatherlyn walked in, there was no greeting. When my father entered, he was greeted. My family was vigilantly watched all the time we were in the store.

Toward the end of the South Dakota portion of the trip, Heatherlyn started to have a panic attack. I pulled over, and we walked up and down the rural gravel road for a while processing the many racist encounters of the past several days and their potential impact on our sons. This deepened my understanding of the cumulative weight of the gazes that she experiences daily. Through the years, I have seen it change her. It is no longer so easy to blow off a racist stare, saying, "Maybe he just thought I was beautiful." It is not so easy for me to be polite when my family or others I care about experience racism.

Through the years, there were many times where I heard my father say, "We really love Heather" with tears in his eyes. While emotions were not his forte, he was more proficient in the expression of emotion in the form of sentimentality. These tears were a testimony to the depth of his love. The same would happen with my sons. There was never wonder about his love for my family; it could be seen. He cared about Heatherlyn's family, too. He spoke fondly of her brothers, parents, and other relatives he met. He would ask with interest about how they are doing. If you knew my father well, you could sense when his questions and comments went beyond the surface pleasantries. You knew when they came from a place of love.

While your behavior and unwillingness to acknowledge my wife warrants hurt and anger, I know my emotions are about more than your callous behavior; it is also about what you symbolize. My father thought he had largely overcome the racism that he grew up with and was surprised by some of his feelings when I started dating Heatherlyn. I know that he wanted to rid himself of any bias, conscious or unconscious. But it was not so easy to do. In a culture where racism abounds, none of us grow up unscathed. Yet never would my father engage in or condone the type of behavior you displayed, even before his growth.

My father did not want to feel he had to confront racism. Many times, I became angry at his hesitance to be more vocal against racism. He was an influential person and maybe his voice could have made a difference where my voice could not. While I wanted him to stand for justice and what is right, more than that I wanted him to stand up for me and my family.

The no handshake and no acknowledgement are profound symbols of my father's struggle. Your presence and your choice not to acknowledge Heatherlyn's existence was representative of one of my father's deepest struggles. It would have made him uncomfortable, but he would have believed this was not the time or place to address it. At the viewing, I would have likely agreed.

I, too, struggle about when to confront situations and when not to. The most common microaggression Heatherlyn and I experience, and sometimes our family experiences, is the comment, "Will that be one check or two?" I am sure that many would respond saying, "How do you know that is racism?" I do not. Yet, many times I have listened as the same person gives the check to other tables with other couples without the question. One time, we even received this question after a couple's massage! If isolated, these incidents would be easy to laugh off. But after years of marriage, the pebbles carry the same weight as a large boulder.

Maybe if still alive my father would have found a way to confront your behavior at a later time. Maybe he would have buried his discomfort. While my hope is the former, my guess is the latter. Either way, he would have been hurt by your actions. I wonder how you would have felt had my father witnessed a similar behavior while alive and found a way to calmly address this with you. Would it have made a difference? Would you have felt the shame that you ought to feel? Even if knowing he could not confront you about what happened at his funeral, surely you know that he would not have approved of what you did.

After my sons were born, my father hoped that they would not have to worry about being treated differently because of who they were. This was a complex reality. In part, he hoped my privilege would protect them. But he also hoped that being lighter skinned and educated would protect them. This was a mixture of naïveté, optimism, limited understanding of racism, and unwillingness to acknowledge aspects of how difficult it would be for his grandchildren. The eternal optimist in him sometimes prevented him from seeing the world as it is, and his powers of denial were strong. This is a luxury I do not have if I am to be as good a father to my sons as he was to me. I must be willing to protect them.

I must be willing to protect my sons from people like you; from people who will come to the viewing of my father and not shake my wife's hand. The responsibility to stand up for my family and others who share similar identities does not feel like a burden to me. But the realities that create this necessity are as painful a burden as I have ever had to carry.

Likely, you do not know that your behavior was noticed. Maybe you do not care. I am sure that you are not aware of the pain and anger that it caused many of us in your friend's family—including my mother, whom one of you hugged. It is unlikely you will ever read these words. I do not know if you would recognize yourself in them or if it would make a difference. I do not know if you would repent or feel more strident in what you view as righteous anger. If someday you attend my mother's viewing, I do not know if you would change your behavior after reading these words or maybe choose not to attend. If you do attend and ignore my family's existence, I may not be silent.

Sincerely,
Louis Hoffman

Letter 21
Heatherlyn[1]

Heatherlyn,

Your relationship with my father was complicated, as was mine, which often pained me. When you first met him, he struggled and did not handle it well—remaining silent as an expression of his discomfort. While later I came to recognize that he had deep shame about his struggle, it did not change that you were hurt by this first meeting. My anger at him, along with empathy and sadness for you, was a powerful and complex combination of emotions that I had to sort through. At that time, I had never really confronted my father about anything; I held him in too high esteem to even consider that seriously. During the weeks after the meeting, I have vivid memories of pacing my living room, pleading with him over the phone to get into therapy to work on the prejudice behind his reaction.

I no longer remember if it was before or after this meeting that you told me, "Just let him get to know me." Even though you were hurt by my father's actions, it appeared you had more patience than I did—and you were right. With time, you came to recognize this was also partially to comfort me at your own emotional toll. As my father got to know you, of course, he grew very fond of you. This is something that I have witnessed repeatedly. People like you and are drawn to you. I remember a friend commenting once that if anyone did not like you, there was obviously something wrong with them. Among the very few people who did not like you, the "wrong with them" was consistently evident, most frequently in the form of racism.

My father's struggle with racism was one of the first prominent encounters with racism during our relationship. But it laid a painful seed. While my father worked to address his racism, even though imperfectly and incompletely, it did not remove the wound.

---

[1] Although this letter was written by Louis, Heatherlyn reviewed it for accuracy and to approve the content.

Early in our relationship, I was more aware of the racism that we encountered than you. In part, this was because you grew up a person of majority in the Bahamas. Racism was not as prevalent in your experience before we met. Conversely, I grew up seeing "behind the curtain," witnessing the racism that White people will often only show other White people in private spaces. I noticed the looks we would get, how we were ignored when ring shopping, and many other microaggressions. And I would get mad. You, at first, seemed to be able to just brush it off, often with humor.

When our relationship began, I was aware that dating you, and later marrying you, would reveal some people's racism and end some friendships. Any stand for social justice, whether in one's personal or professional life, requires that one be ready to challenge and even lose some relationships. Although I had too little experience to deeply understand this at the time, my intuition and integrity were guiding me toward this recognition. There was sadness and anxiety about this, wondering who might be involved, but this was no deterrent. It was clear these were people I would not want in prominent positions in my life anyway. The self-reflection taught me about myself. It concerned me that I did not know some people well enough to see their racism before dating you made it evident.

Through our first years of marriage, I wanted to make sure you knew that you were my priority. I loved my family, and preserving those relationships was important. But you were my first priority. Yet, in the early years, I was often clumsy, and my intentions did not always come through clearly. It also took me time to work up the courage and to find my voice. I put things off and avoided them at times, which wounded you. You often guided me through this process. It was easier to find my voice in other settings such as work and with friends. Working through the complexities of a biracial extended family is challenging. Shortly after our second son was born, I found my footing. By this time, there were some wounds from me added to the wounds from my father. These wounds—these sins of omission from not finding my courage and voice with my family early enough—will always carry some guilt with me.

When I reflect on our years together, there are so many ways I can join my father's chorus of "we are blessed." One of the greatest gifts, though, is that I know—definitively—that I am a better person for you being in my life. There are many reasons for this, including the direct impact you have upon me and how my love for you has inspired me, giving me courage to confront problems in the world in which we live.

When I witnessed the impact of racism and the world upon you, I wanted to make it better for you.

When we first met, one of the most powerful things drawing me to you was your courageous and beautiful vulnerability, and your acceptance of my vulnerability. Your vulnerability was tied to a strength and resilience that enhanced its glow. The coexistence of vulnerability, strength, and courage is one that I find very attractive. Yet, it seems that I have been forced to watch as the world took this away from you. It changed you, and I felt helpless to do anything about it except trying to understand and comfort you when you would let me. But this was not enough. It seems you learned that the United States, in the time in which we were living, could be a dangerous place for a Black woman to be vulnerable. So this beauty slipped away to a more hidden and protected place, one that I could not always find even when diligently searching.

I know you were not merely a victim, and it was not merely the world. After our sons were born, when what my friend Glen Moriarty called "Daddy juice" kicked in, I became very focused on work and finances. Those first couple years after Lakoda was born, I sometimes lost track of you as my first priority, and I was not always there for you. My regret for this has never left after it was recognized. You made choices, too, and sometimes those choices were to protect yourself first. I cannot blame you for that as you navigated this new world you had not planned or prepared for.

There is such as sense of powerlessness that has been part of being in a biracial relationship. There are so many pains and injustices that cannot be avoided or overcome. Watching what has transpired in the world over the last 8−10 years has been crushing. One of the powerful symbols of this was walking on a rural road in South Dakota. Our family had experienced many incidents of racism on the trip across South Dakota, including several when visiting my father's hometown a few minutes before this walk. As we drove off toward Minnesota, it became too much, and your anxiety burst through in a panic attack. I pulled over, and we walked that gravel road and talked, with me rubbing your back until the anxiety eased. Another scar had formed. Later, I cried for your wound, and I cried for the protections that you seemed to have reinforced to keep you safe from the world—protections I never had to learn for myself.

Heatherlyn, I love you, and I hate how the world has sometimes impacted you. Some days I want to rage at the world on your behalf. I hate that I could not protect you or heal you, even though I know that is not my job. My job is to love you. I have tried my best to fill this role and to continually embrace this pursuit with humility and courage, even if imperfectly so. Being the good enough husband was not good enough for me—but all that was within the realm of possibility.

As my father's end approached, I know that you were not able to see some of the progress my father made. It was revealed selectively, and you were not privy to it. This was something that I had not fully realized until after my father was gone. It added a layer to the grieving process for me, and I know it has for you as well. In Iowa, it was not easy. You were the only Black woman, and our sons the only Black people. Even at the viewing and the funeral, you could not fully exhale. There were too many eyes on you, and it was never clear who might not want to shake your hand or acknowledge your existence. While I recognized that my protective and comforting instincts emerged at times, I was in my own grief and focused on my mother. There were a few places like Reynold's, my favorite clothing store, where the hypervigilance could be lowered. It was an unfair context for us to grieve while you were still figuring out your relationship with my father and how to handle the related grief.

When we first started dating, I began conceiving of my ideal relationship, viewing it as one of continual growth together as well as supporting each other's personal growth. This was a foundation of relational depth, mutuality, and the commitment to each other. I have tried to never sway from that, although I know there were some periods in the early days of parenthood when I lost sight of this. Still, rarely if ever is there a week where I do not come out of a therapy session, supervision session, class, journaling session, or some other relational or intellectual engagement where I have not found some inspiration to try to be a better spouse, father, professor, supervisor, and/or friend. These are not always actualized, but I revel in this process, this opportunity to grow. I hope I never lose this zeal for growth. The desire to be better for you has been a primary inspiration emerging from these other places of relational depth, reflection, and intellectual engagement. You may not always witness it coming to fruition, but I hope you can see in some way that this process has lived in me and always will. It has become part of my way of being that I treasure. To be sure, without you, it would not have the vibrancy that it has had in my life.

With appreciation and love,
Louis

Letter 22
A Letter to My Father's Political Colleagues

To My Father's Political Colleagues, Republican and Democrat,

There was much my father and I did not agree about politically. He was a Republican who served in the Iowa House of Representatives for 10 years. I do not like the two-party system and would align more with progressive politics than conservative. Despite our differences, he was a great model of integrity in politics.

One story my father told about politics demonstrates his integrity most clearly. When he was first in office, after a significant event in Iowa or the country happened, the parties would get together and talk about what was best for Iowa. He said this changed during his time in the legislature. Toward the end of his tenure, when something impactful happened, he believed the parties would get together to discuss what would make them look good and the other party look bad. When this change occurred, he said it was time for him to leave his role in the House.

John and I went to Des Moines to listen to his final talk in the House chambers. It was an interesting, and telling, event. As we spent the day around my father's colleagues, many came up and introduced themselves. The Republicans tended to be tentative in their appreciation for my father, which surprised me. By all accounts, my father was one of the most influential Republicans in Western Iowa, and really all of Iowa, for several years. He was even recruited several times to run for governor but always declined. His Democrat colleagues were warmer, more genuine, and enthusiastic in their praise of my father.

In trying to make sense of this, it seemed one primary factor was the most plausible reason for more genuine appreciation of my father from the "other" party. My father believed in, and lived, working across party lines to do what was best for Iowa and our country. He believed in compromise and collaboration. Iowa and the country had moved in a direction where it was party over country, something that has worsened. This deeply saddened my father. I hope it will change, but I am not optimistic.

My father and I talked about politics often. As his dementia appeared following COVID, we spoke less frequently. It was apparent that as he began experiencing the cognitive decline, he started to rely on more extreme, partisan sources, and his critical thinking was compromised. It was no longer productive to have conversations about politics because he no longer possessed the cognitive abilities to think broadly and critically about important issues. This was hard to watch. But I knew this was not a reflection of the values that governed his life. Rather, it was a product of the health issues he was facing.

At his best, my father strove to listen and see both sides. When in the legislature, he explained that each weekend alone he would receive over 100 emails, and each week he would receive large stacks of mail. This did not include all the bills and other materials he had to read. It was not realistic to thoroughly read everything and be as informed as he wanted to be. Due to this, he said he had to rely on experts, lobbyists, and information from his party at times. Again, this was not ideal, which he recognized. But it was hard to avoid.

My father also listened. This was something I appreciated when I had the chance to observe. When he was talking to people about political issues, he intently listened and considered what people were saying, whether or not he agreed with them. He believed it was part of the job of a leader to listen, and he did it well.

On several occasions, my father consulted with me about issues related to mental health. This was not his area of expertise. He would tell me what he was thinking based on the information he was given. I helped him understand the different sides of the issue, which he always appreciated. He would often change his mind and approach on issues following our conversations. Politicians with integrity should change their mind at times. To be resistant to changing one's opinion is not a sign of character, but problematic ego, a lack of critical thinking, or being closed-minded. None of these are a sign of a good political leader.

I learned important lessons from this, too. Psychologists, counselors, and social workers have much less political power compared to psychiatrists, medical doctors, and pharmaceutical companies. This is primarily due to financial reasons. Psychologists, counselors, and social workers do not make as much money or have access to the same financial resources. Because of this, our voices are often not heard as clearly. This helped me recognize the importance of speaking out about mental health issues as a psychologist.

I also learned the complexities of some issues. Without giving away my father's secrets, I know there were views that he held that he would not share publicly and not necessarily vote consistent with. If he voted against the party line on some issues, he was aware that it could cost him political influence and potentially impact his ability to be re-elected. As we discussed one of these issues, he said that he just stayed silent on these issues publicly. When a vote came up on these issues, if it was clear how the vote was going to go, he would try not to vote or to abstain; however, sometimes he would vote with his party knowing that it would not alter the outcome. When he voted with the party, he did so without speaking on the issue; it was a passive assent to what was inevitable. However, he said if the vote was close and his vote might be the deciding vote, then he would vote for what he believed was right.

I am sure people will have mixed reactions to this. Some may view this as my father compromising his integrity by not speaking out. Others may be disappointed in the political system and how corrupt it has become. These are understandable reactions. However, to my knowledge, my father did not speak against what he believed. He was pragmatic. He knew certain votes or speaking out on certain issues could negatively affect his ability to make an impact on other issues.

My father also talked about the complexity of politics, which is something many do not recognize. It needs to be discussed more. At times, he might agree with much of a bill but vote against it because of aspects of the bill that he disagreed with. The media too often presents bills as if they were simple and straightforward. They may, for example, say a politician voted against supporting veterans; however, they may have agreed with the part of the bill supporting veterans but could not support it because of other aspects of the bill or the way it was supporting veterans. My father, at least with me, tried to be transparent about these issues. We need more of this type of transparency in the public eye.

Valuable lessons about the political process were gained from conversations with my father. I recognize more deeply how hard your jobs are as Representatives, Senators, Governors, and in other political positions. There are smear campaigns, which my father experienced a few times. There are complexities that are not recognized, distorted, or oversimplified by the media or general public. There is a realistic challenge at times between voting your conscience versus voting for what the people in your district would want.

The general public needs to be educated about these issues, and we need greater transparency from politicians. But most of all, we need politicians who will put state and country before party. We need politicians who will listen to one another and the general public. We need politicians with the type of integrity that my father showed in all political parties. While I have strong political beliefs myself, I have more respect and appreciation for politicians from any party that can demonstrate the integrity my father did than I do for politicians who greatly align with my political beliefs but do not have integrity.

Though my father is gone, I hope that you can learn from his legacy. More than that, I hope you can be inspired, maybe even challenged by it, so that you can pursue a better political reality than the one we are facing today.

Sincerely,
Louis Hoffman

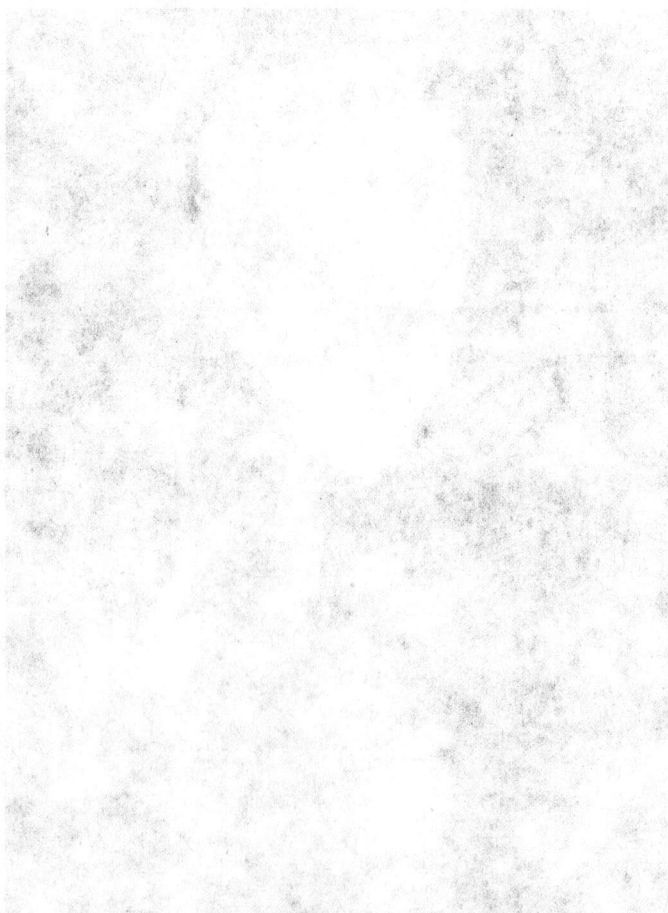

Part 4

Your Love

Letter 23
"There's My Pretty Girl"

Dad,

"There's my pretty girl." Not your last words, but your last sentence. I could not have asked for a more perfect final sentence. I know you loved Mom. I saw this so many times and in so many ways. It was not always the ways that Mom needed to hear it, but they were genuine expressions of your love. Mom knew this, too.

As Mom told me you said this just a few hours before you were gone, the beauty with which she treasured these words was palpable. Even saying, "I love you, babe," as you often did, would not have meant as much. Mom joked that for the first 20 years of your marriage she would have loved to have heard those words that were so rarely spoken. Your ways of communicating love did not always align, as is often the case. But over time, you found ways to make it known, even if Mom held on to some sadness at not hearing some of the expressions of love she longed for.

I had witnessed your testimonies of love of many times. I had no doubt of the depth of your love and commitment to Mom. But as much as I yearned for that last smile and relished hearing my name, I wanted this for Mom even more. As I heard her talk of this, it was some of the clearest moments of joy that broke up her grief. Thank you, Dad, for giving Mom this final gift.

With appreciation,
Louis

Letter 24
Standing by Mom

Dad,

Around 2012, Mom became very sick with a knee infection. While my family was at Disneyland, we received the call from you that Mom was in the ER and being taken to a hospital in Omaha. We ended our vacation early, drove back to Northern California, where we were living at the time, and I flew to Omaha. My job allowed me to be remote at that time, so I was able to be there for as long as needed.

They had induced Mom into a coma due to the severity of the pain beginning to shut down her organs, and she was not coming out. It was not clear if she would survive. When I arrived, Mom was still in a coma. Although you were still regularly working 50–60 hours weeks at this time, you stayed at her side in Omaha. While I was back, you would sometimes take a day to go back to Iowa to get some work and clothes but then returned.

I traveled to Omaha a couple of times while Mom was in the hospital. Working from her hospital room grew to feel almost normal. That summer I was preparing to begin my term as president of the Society for Humanistic Psychology. As the convention and one of our big meetings approached, I made calls from her hospital room trying to fill a vacancy on the board and prepare the meeting agenda. You, too, worked from her room or your hotel room, but you always made sure to be there when the doctors were doing their rounds. You did not want to miss that.

When you were working from your room or taking a day trip back to Iowa, the nurses and doctors would tell me that you did not need to be there all the time and that few would stay night after night. In part, you could do this because of your privilege. You could afford the hotel room and work from Omaha. Each night, we would go for dinner, exploring different restaurants in Omaha. This was self-care for you as you loved to eat out and Denison did not have the options of the bigger city. I enjoyed these dinners. You were a bit more open, and your love for Mom was evident. Never before was I as certain of your love for Mom as while she was in the hospital.

To witness your love was meaningful. As someone who feels love deeply, I did not always see the depth of your love for Mom. I recognized that you were not always present, and she sometimes struggled with how much you were away. This made it more meaningful to see your commitment during this time. It was a witness that I wanted to take in so that I could live such a love as well.

Love,
Louis

My parents at their wedding, December 28, 1968

Letter 25
A Letter to My Mother

Mom,

As we prepared together for Dad's death, I worried more for you than for me. He was well over a decade older than you, so I often wondered how long you had been preparing for this. After all, you had to know that most likely he would die well before you did even when accepting his marriage proposal.

One of my favorite songs is "Dance with My Father" by Luther Vandross.[1] For years, I have cried through much of this song. Without fail, I cry the hardest when he sings about crying for his mother more than for himself. The thought of you grieving for Dad often hurt as much as my own grief.

Several months ago, when I was visiting home, I shared with you that I worried that you always felt that you, too, lived in Dad's shadow. When young, John and I idolized (and idealized) Dad. As I grew older, he became more human to me, and I was able to see you more clearly. While I see both of you in me, at this point in my life I see more of you than him. Your compassion, creativity, sensitivity, and openness to greater relational depth are more aligned with the person whom I have become. I am thankful for the gifts I have received from both of you.

Dad had a big presence. There were many wonderful things in this, but, at times, you were lost in this presence. There are beautiful parts of who you are that have been hidden. You have shared some stories about your early relationship with Dad. Given how and when he was raised, he had taken on strong assumptions about the role of a husband and wife that were closely aligned with patriarchy. Over the years, he did much to rethink this—in part because you made him. Yet, I do not think that you give yourself credit for this.

When growing up, I was not able to see the ways that you influenced Dad. Now, I can see the myriads of ways that he was a better man, and

---

[1] Vandross, L., & Marx, R. (2003). Dance with my father [Recorded by L. Vandross]. On *Dance with my father* [Album]. J.

a better father, because of you. This continued well after John and I had families of our own. You helped him be a better grandfather, too. I am thankful for the father and grandfather you helped him become.

Our relationship has been much closer than my relationship with Dad was since I became an adult. While when I needed to talk about financial struggles or stress, I turned to Dad, for most of the rest there was more comfort and connection talking with you. We were able to have the talks that elicited tears from the depths of feeling, which could not be had with Dad.

I hope that you are able to become the person you want to be in this phase of life. Typing these words brings some trepidation, as they could easily be misinterpreted. This is not intended as a criticism of Dad, but rather a recognition and celebration of you.

You have always been a wonderful mother and grandmother. When Lakoda was young, he often seemed obsessed with you. His love for you was so evident. Later, Lukaya and Lyon, too, were very close to you. It was one of my great joys to see the excitement and contentment on their faces when you would play games, read, or cuddle with them. I would always try to get a picture of these moments. While I did not get them all, we have a lot of pictures of you with them!

While rural Iowa could never be my home again, I hate that it is so far from where I am. The last couple of years, but particularly the last seven months, Colorado has felt too far from Iowa. It is hard not to be able to be there for you whenever needed. When you were sick and in a coma for a couple of weeks, I remember vividly and viscerally several times where I had the urge to call you, then broke down crying realizing that I could not. I can still feel the pain of those moments, and my eyes well with tears typing these words.

I love you, Mom. And I loved Dad. I wish that I could give you a few more days with him at home in the sunroom or on the deck, having steaks and wine. I wish I could hear him say to you a few more times, "I love you, babe."

Love,
Louis

Letter 26
Mentoring

Dad,

At the visitation and funeral, it became clearer to me that you were viewed as a mentor to many. Many people looked up to you and claimed you as their mentor. While this was evident before your death, the depth and breadth of your impact became more evident as I heard people share about how you impacted them. Listening to these stories, I could not help but wonder what the experience of mentorship with you was like. While I have some idea from being your son, this remains mysterious to me as well. Part of me longed to have been able to have that experience with you—or at least witness it.

Mentoring has become a deeply meaningful role to me. I still remember some of the first few times someone referred to me as their mentor and feeling the shock of it. I felt too young to be a mentor—still often do. Several years ago four current and former students wrote an article about me in a special issue of a journal, *NeuroQuantology*, "Pioneers Who Have Changed the Face of Science and Those That Have Been Mentored by Them."[1] I was surprised, then later feared my shock could have been interpreted as a lack of appreciation. Paradoxically, I see myself in mentoring roles but not as a mentor. Maybe this is my impostor syndrome. While always being surprised, I also think of being called a mentor as one of the most meaningful compliments that I could receive. Mentoring is more than teaching, supervising, or guiding; it entails a deep relationship and impact, hopefully mutual. Often, on both sides of my experience of mentoring, it has turned into a deep friendship, too.

On the drive home from your funeral, my thoughts returned to wondering what type of mentor you were, how similar and different our styles were, and what I could have learned from you to become a better mentor. It is a conversation I wish we could have had in the living

---

[1] Dias, J., Claypool, T. Moats, M. & Hoxie, E. (2011). Louis Hoffman and the art of international dialogue. *NeuroQuantology, 9,* 530-534.

years. Yet had I asked you about your approach to mentoring people, I suspect you may not have thought of yourself as a mentor—maybe your own insecurities or imposter syndrome. Listening, being supportive, and modeling, I am sure, would be qualities that your mentees would identify in you. But what else?

Early in my career, I experienced two very different approaches to mentorship. One person, whom I never claimed or wanted as a mentor, was intent on me identifying him as my mentor. He even told others that I sought him out as a mentor, though I had never said this myself. He wanted me to be like him. Not only did I not want to be like him or mentor under him, but I did also not like this approach to mentoring. My two other mentors, Robert Murney and Myrtle Heery, never would assume mentorship. This is part of why I was drawn to them. Both wanted to help me become the person, and the professional, that I wanted to become. They were not in search of a "mini-me" but rather approached mentorship generatively.

Although I do not know much about your relationship with people that saw you as a mentor, there is confidence that you never tried to pressure them to be like you. Rather, you saw potential in them, were proud of them, and wanted to support them becoming the best person and professional they could be. You may have hoped for them to take on particular values and approaches, but you would not have forced them to follow your way. I know this, in part, because I also experienced this from you.

In college, I thought I wanted to become an accountant. It was not an insurance salesman, but it was something in business. This seemed to make you happy—maybe because it was a similar field. We spoke of ways that you could help me get started in accounting, including a friend of yours I might be able to train under and eventually take over his business. But that first year in college I was falling asleep in my business classes. I even received my first and only C in business class. My draw to psychology was growing and my childhood desire to be a writer was reinvigorated. The college I was at did not have a writing major, so I majored in psychology and theology with a writing minor, eventually dropping the minor. As my path diverged from anything along the lines of business, your support never flinched. I never felt any pressure to follow a path resembling yours.

Now, as a mid-career psychologist, I find myself in roles often associated with mentoring. As a teacher and supervisor, I often think of the Nietzsche quote, "One repays a teacher badly if one always remains nothing but a pupil."[2] While this could be interpreted in various ways, the meaning for me is that a student must become their own person, not merely a reflection of their mentor. Divergence does not dishonor the mentor but rather is a reflection that the mentor has done their job well. The other side of Nietzsche's quote is that if a teacher pressures a student to remain their student or protege, they dishonor their student.

When I was a full professor in a graduate program in psychology, I was placed in roles that encouraged students to see me as their mentor. While I enjoy teaching and supervising, mentoring is an even deeper passion because it is about supporting the whole person of the student and being embedded in a deeper relationship. It is investing in the student's success and life journey, through as well as beyond the teaching or supervising roles. While it can be part of teaching and supervising, it is not always the case. At the last place I taught full time, the workloads grew so great that there was little time for mentorship. I was even told by two administrators that I should not invest as much in doing a good job, but this is not who I am or want to be.

I have often said that I left academia to be an academic. I meant many things by this, but there were two primary meanings. I left academia so I would have time to engage in scholarly writing. During my last several years of teaching the only time for this was late at night or an occasional weekend when I was not grading. The even more meaningful aspect of this was that I left academia to have more time for students. As an adjunct, while not teaching as much, I could invest to a greater degree in teaching, supervising, and mentoring. Whenever a student says to me, "I know you are busy. . ." a sadness grows in me. While there is appreciation for the respect of my time, I do not ever want this to prevent a student from reaching out. It would be preferable to sometimes have to say that I do not have time for something than to have them not ask for it out of consideration for me being busy.

Now I teach one class a year and occasionally an additional class. I also provide clinical supervision at one of the universities where I teach. At the nonprofit where I serve as executive director, we have developed a clinic where I provide much of the supervision. This provides a place with more opportunities for the mentoring role. Since your funeral, there has been a stronger pull toward these mentoring roles. In my reflection, I see a variety of reasons for this shift.

---

[2] Nietzsche, F. (1954). *Thus spoke Zarathustra: A book for none and all* (W. Kaufmann, Trans.). Penguin, p. 78. (Original work published 1892)

What is most essential to me in these roles is being generative. From what I can tell, you did not have expectations contingent upon your mentorship. You offered it because it was who you were, and it was meaningful to you. Anything that came back to you from the mentorship was a blessing, not an expectation. You loved to say you were blessed. I hope this is one of the ways that those blessings came to you.

It was evident that you gave of yourself, and you gave people opportunities. This is an aspect of your mentoring I long to know more about. When I am impressed with a student or early career person, I seek to create opportunities for them that can help them advance their career, particularly toward goals or excitements they may have. At times, I recognize I overdo this. Although in a different context, a friend, Michael Moats, and I have done many projects together. We joked about my proclivity to come up with ideas for books and other meaningful projects. This is why Mike sometimes will answer the phone when I call by just saying "no." In recent years, I have begun warning students that I may offer too many opportunities, and it is okay to say "no." If they struggle with this, I tell them the story of Mike and offer to connect them with him for some "saying-no consultations."

There were costs you paid for seeking to help others and support their dreams. But I never heard you complain about these costs. This seems a place of similarity that I never was able to get to know about you. Curiosities remain about what I could have learned from you with our shared desire to support the dreams of people in whom we see potential.

There were, without doubt, divergences in our mentoring styles. It is unlikely that you prioritized relational depth or creating opportunities for others, which seem to be rather natural aspects of my approach. However, I know you cared for people who saw you as their mentor, even to the point of taking risks investing in them. You also protected them, which was evident from many stories shared through the years. I feel that protectiveness, too. Many of your mentee relationships over time evolved into friendships, which is something that I have been blessed to have happen as well.

My approach to being a teacher, mentor, and father has surely been influenced by you—even more than I know. Through these roles there is a continued sense of connection with you. For that, I am thankful. Even more, I am blessed.

Your proud son and mentee,
Louis

Letter 27
"What Did Your Parents Do Right?"

Dad,

When Heatherlyn and I were dating, and John and Joy had already married, a Latina friend asked me, "What did your parents do right?" She was referring to both John and I marrying women of color. Her words were not suggesting that it was better to marry a woman of color than a White woman, but rather that we were open to it. I had never considered this, but her question deeply impacted me. It is a question that I have thought about for many years without fully knowing the answer. I do not imagine that this is a question ever to be fully answered, but it is still meaningful to explore.

I have no memories of Mom saying or doing anything that would be perceived as racist when I was growing up. With you, the closest I remember is you occasionally saying it was nice when a sports team had a good number of White players doing well on the team. This was a microaggressive statement; however, I did not interpret this as suggesting anything negative about people of color. That did not seem your tone; nor was it your intention.[1] As an adult, the memories of these comments have bothered me. My awareness and situatedness in the world have changed.

Racism was prevalent in our community but did not make sense to me growing up—which it does not to most children and youth. There were few people of color in our school, community, or even nearby towns. I was not exposed to much racial diversity. The implicit message taken from you not participating in the racism around us was that it was not okay and that you and Mom accepted people from different racial backgrounds. Neither of you had many experiences in diverse contexts either, limiting your awareness and understanding. While the conversations about race were missing, there is no doubt that had John or I ever engaged in racism we would have had a conversation letting us know this was not okay.

---

[1] Microaggressions, while harmful, are unintentional and may even be well-intentioned.

For John and me to both marry women of color, it seems there must have been something more. I am sure that part of this was embedded in the messages of compassion. You showed concern for people, including people who were struggling or different. Other people who were judged by many in our community you did not judge or speak ill of, and you even showed them compassion. If you were to speak ill of someone, it was likely because they spoke ill of others.

The messages of acceptance were implicit. They were modeled. It was not until much later that I learned of your own struggles, which were struggles you did not wish to have. Although there was awareness entering the relationship that Heatherlyn and I would encounter a lack of acceptance from many, I did not expect you to have difficulty accepting me being in a biracial relationship. Some of your struggles came from your early experiences with your family and community as a child, adolescent, and young adult. It seems that you did not want to pass them on to John and me. While you never completed your own work, somehow you prevented the transmission of your struggles to your children.

Being in a biracial relationship is not always easy, and a White man being married to a Black woman is one of the rarer couplings. While there are the challenges of merging different cultures, this was not the most difficult part. We managed this pretty well. Dealing with the looks, judgments, and microaggressions is much more difficult. Heatherlyn, growing up as a person of majority in the Bahamas, did not encounter this directly either. We have experienced years of racism and microaggressions, both direct experience and witnessing it all around us, that have changed both of us. This is some of what you worried about, but your worry was not necessary—and this worry even hurt. These changes in myself have been fully embraced and appreciated. While they came with pain and scars, these have made me a better person and a better therapist.

Being married to a Black woman has introduced a painful source of alienation in life. Pondering this alienation has become a source of growth and strength. I recognize that no matter the love for my family, I can never know their experience or escape the privileges that come with being White. There is a gulf that can never be crossed. With my White friends, even when they are deeply aware of racial disparities and the impact of racism, there remains an unbridgeable gulf as well. This one tends to come with more angst. Even with their desire to understand, they are not able to cross over the chasm separating us.

The alienation of being in a biracial relationship[2] is painful, but blessing can be made from the pain. It has changed my sense of self. With some experiences in my life, there is no one with whom I can turn where that deeper resonance is present. Facing this directly has helped me discover how to use my privilege in ways that protect my family. It has required me to become more courageous, willing to see things others choose not to see and take stands others choose not to take. These changes have blessed me; they have given me gifts of wisdom, courage, and compassion. This has helped me impact the world and others in ways that would not have been possible without this experience. But I worry when people enter these relationships without considering how it will change them or without the right intentions.

Seeing an interracial couple or marriage often brings out varied emotions in me. My first reaction is almost always appreciation, which has, at times, led to my gazing at biracial couples a bit too long. Without doubt, there were some encounters on the street where Heatherlyn was not with me where the couple likely spoke of the racist White guy staring at them. When seeing these couples, I sometimes feel hope in the possibility of overcoming my sense of alienation.

I have not been a perfect husband and am still trying to be better. As a guilt-prone person, my years in existential psychology have helped me embrace and value guilt. The guilt of being an imperfect spouse and imperfect father are the guilts most difficult to bear and appreciate. As husbands go, I believe I have been a pretty good spouse, but that is not enough for me. The place where I have some pride, maybe even arrogance, is that as a biracial spouse I have done quite well. There are still blinds spots, and I can, and often do, share times when my blind spots have led to hurt. While there is pride in being a good biracial spouse, there is also recognition that much of this is because my parents did something well—even if I cannot identify what that was.

There is a potential shadow side to this pride, too. Through the years, I have witnessed many White partners in biracial relationships who, sometimes despite good intentions, have not done it well. Within myself, I recognize a protectiveness in some encounters with biracial relationships. This protectiveness is a worry that the White partner will not do it well, will cause harm to their spouse and to their children because of the lack of courage to face the realities of racism and its

---

[2] In this letter, "biracial" generally referring to a biracial relationship in which one partner is White. For readability and to avoid excess wordiness, this has not been written out explicitly with each reference to a biracial relationship.

implications directly. One cannot fight racism and be unscathed; courage and strength are needed. All White spouses in biracial relationships will make mistakes and cause harm. This is part of our humanness. However, my protectiveness emerges when encountering a couple where it is not evident that the White partner has the courage and strength to do the self-explorations and take the stands needed for these relationships.

The idealizations in the early phases of love or infatuation can make it hard to see this lack of deeper courage in oneself or one's partner. For one thing, the early stages of love bolstered by the newness of relationships can give a false appearance of courage that will not sustain. Eventually, the White partner may want to return to being seen as nice, avoiding conflict and enjoying the comfort of their privileges. It can also cover blind spots, as love always does. My mentor, Robert Murney, was fond of saying, "We always marry our idealized image of our partner, then sometime after the wedding vows we meet the person we married." While this is almost always true, the implications of this can be more profound in interracial relationships.

At times over the past several years, I have enjoyed following some interracial couples on social media, particularly White men married to Black women. These help me feel less alienated, and the common use of humor to disarm the tension when talking about difficult topics is something that I appreciate. But there are videos or posts that elicit a cringe. At times, it is evident that the White spouse still, in ways, looks down on their partner, seeing them as less-than. They may truly love their partner, but this love may be rooted partially in a belief that they are inferior, subservient, or easily molded, even manipulated. At other times, the White spouse seems lacking the courage or awareness to take stands. While I want to see more interracial relationships and often feel a deep connection when encountering others in these relationships, it is important to me that the White spouse is willing to rise to the necessary challenges and has the courage and awareness to be a good partner. They must embrace the full humanness and beauty of their partner, and in this be willing to face the realities of the world directly.

For many years, there has been a desire within me to focus on couples therapy with biracial couples and engage in research on biracial couples. I previously worried about my ability to be objective, and the potential of my expectations of White spouses to come through. Also, I recognize there is a problematic paternalistic element with my protectiveness. This is evidence that I still have some of my own work to do. Although very different, I have felt the pain of paternalism in these contexts. You were trying to protect me, your White son, and I have an impulse to defend or protect the partner who is not White. While facilitating the development of awareness is vital, the protectiveness is sometimes not my role as a couple's therapist.

The interest in research on biracial couples is a bit different. Diverse motivations draw me to this research, including to see if my ponderings are justified, to better understand these relationships, and to help people in biracial relationships and their families. My draw toward this research is also rooted in a desire to feel less alone and to learn to be a better partner and father.

If my sons someday have a partner who is White, it will be important for me to be aware of my biases. While it involves very different aspects, I may have some work to do that bears some similarity to the work you had to do. This is a possibility that I ought to prepare for.

As death prompts reflections on death and I have watched Mom grieve you, there are times in the weeks since you have been gone where I have reflected on how I would manage if anything happened to Heatherlyn. The grief aspects are better for my journal. However, I have considered this in the more distal context of being thrown back into being single after a biracial marriage. With my biases, changed sense of self, and three biracial sons, there is a recognition that it would be difficult to pursue a new romantic relationship. Hopefully, this is a reality that I will not have to face.

In looking at my own reflections on interracial relationships, I am drawn to wondering how these relate to your struggles. When I told you I was getting close to a Black woman and interested in dating her, you did not rise to the occasion, and it hurt. Through our conversations, I know some of your concerns bear similarities to my concerns about White partners. Against your will, you were being thrown into a situation you did not choose or want where courage was needed. Despite this, somehow you and Mom prepared me to have this courage.

There is much more to ponder beyond this letter. It is a start to what surely will receive much attention in my journal. In this letter, there is a deep appreciation to you and Mom for preparing me to be a courageous, and hopefully good enough, biracial spouse. There is also recognition for more work plumbing my depths. While the bias and protectiveness are rooted in love and compassion, it is important that they are rooted in a culturally and personally humble love and compassion. The paternalism must be eradicated, at least to the degree where it can be contained through awareness.

Dad, I pushed you to do your work. Sometimes this was with too little patience and compassion. The urgency did not allow for me to recognize that you were trying, and that you wanted any trace of racism to be gone from yourself. It would be inauthentic of me to ever rest from pushing myself to keep doing my own work. This is the call of cultural humility. When cultural humility is wedded with love, compassion, and passion, it requires continual and courageous intrapersonal exploration and action. I want to be worthy and to continue to grow. In that, too, you and Mom deserve some credit, even if I cannot fully understand it.

I am thankful for this mystery and will gladly carry it with me. My friend was correct that you and Mom did something right. Maybe there is more value and meaning in exploring this question for the rest of my life than there could be in any easy answer. So, thank you, Dad, for the mystery.

Appreciatively,
Louis

My parents

Letter 28
Loving Life

Dad,

One of my favorite philosophers, Simone de Beauvoir, wrote: "Whether you think of it as heavenly or as earthly, if you love life immortality is no consolation for death."[1] The quote is from a book, *A Very Easy Death,* about her mother's last months of life. This quote often came to mind during the several months leading up to your death. You found comfort in your belief in heaven. You also did not want to be kept alive by machines or in a state of constant suffering. But until very close to the end, you kept hope that you would go home to sit in the sunroom and spend another winter season in Florida. You had visions of friends coming by, grilling for them, and having wine and conversation.

Part of this was your optimism. It also was your memory issues that prevented you from knowing the prognosis of your various health issues. Your hope was both inspiring and heart-wrenching. But more than anything else, it was evidence of how much you loved life. Even as your cognitive facilities gradually slipped away, you still loved to sit on the deck or lanai enjoying the view. When I called while you were in one of these spaces, I could hear it in your voice. You did not have to say, "We are blessed" or that you loved life—your voice tone said it all.

When Robert Murney, my friend and mentor, was getting older, and our mentoring relationship transitioned to a deep friendship, we often spoke about death. It bonded us more deeply. His wife, who was already a cancer survivor, was dealing with a potential new cancer. Murney was also thinking more about his own death as he grew older. One day he told me that he was not afraid of death. He was Catholic and, like you, confident that he would go to heaven after dying. From my experience of him telling me this, I believed him. But I was also suspicious.

This conversation was during my early days as an existentialist. At the time, my favorite book was Ernest Becker's *The Denial of Death*.[2] My

---

[1] De Beauvior, S. (1985). *A very easy death*, p. 92. Pantheon.
[2] Becker, E. (1973). *The denial of death* (P. O'Brian, Trans.). Free Press.

conviction was that everyone has fears related to death, even if not of death. While I still tend to believe this, my thinking has become more nuanced, partially from my experience with Murney. As we continued to discuss death, which came up regularly in our conversations, recognition emerged that it was not what would happen after death that he feared; rather, he had a deep sense that he would miss aspects of his life, particularly his wife. This recognition deeply moved me. But it also was a deep love for life and how he was living it. He continued to see clients until shortly before his death when his health deteriorated too much. He loved what he did.

Murney's facing of the end of his life was an inspiration for me. In old age, his focus was on generativity, meaning, and relationship— values we shared, though I was too young to fully appreciate his experience of generativity. I loved Murney and felt his love for me. I still treasure that, and it is no surprise that he has been on my mind again since you died.

There were many ways you are like Murney. You also focused on generativity, meaning, and relationship. You were a giving person who loved what you did and kept working as long as you were able. Murney, however, had done more of "his work," as James Bugental would say. This makes sense. Murney was a psychologist who loved reflection and processing. It was not unusual for him to come into my office, plop down on my couch, and share some new insight he had about himself and his life. If you engaged in this type of self-reflection, you did not share it with others, or at least with me.

In the last six months, as a family we had to make the decision that you were not able to come home. I felt such guilt about this. Not long before, Heatherlyn's family made the same decision about her mother, Helen, who was experiencing more severe dementia than yours that had progressed more rapidly. She had been living with us for a couple of years before the decision was made. I felt that we had failed her. I also felt that I had failed Heatherlyn's family, whom I also dearly love. It was hard to accept that we could not give Helen a better life in our home. Yet, I also recognized that most of each day she was unhappy. I knew that we could not take away her suffering. The cruelness of dementia was more powerful than we were. But maybe we could give her moments of joy. Photographs of good memories and talking with her about the past were the only ways that I seemed to be able to bring about any of these moments of joy.

I felt so powerless to help Helen, especially as she worsened. While as a psychologist I knew it was natural to get frustrated with the situation, I was very hard on myself anytime my frustration with her showed. There were at least four times where I know she recognized my frustration. One was so simple. She could not remember to use the dishwasher as she was not used to such luxuries. For a couple of months, I tried to encourage her to put the dishes in the dishwasher instead of washing them, partially because she could no longer get them adequately clean. Most often, she could not understand and just kept washing the dishes by hand. One day, while she was still sitting at the counter, I took the dishes she had washed and put them in the dishwasher. I saw her embarrassment and sadness. I felt terrible, and from then on waited until she was no longer around to move them from the dish rack to the dishwasher.

Helen has since moved back to the Bahamas. It is better for her to be in her home country, but the guilt and sadness that we could not do more to provide her a better life outside of assisted living remain. This was good preparation for your last months. When Mom was struggling and feeling guilty, I was able to share with her in a more personal (i.e., less clinical) way that we needed to focus on giving you moments of joy. This framework seemed to help Mom. It also helped me.

As family, we were not always on the same page about whether you would be able to come home or needed to be in the nursing home. Although we did not agree, it did not instigate conflict. We discussed it calmly, knowing that we all wanted what is best for you and Mom. Early on, if we could have found 24-hour home care, it would have been possible. But this was not easy to find, and new questions about health issues kept popping up that needed to be addressed before we could really consider it. My hope had been that when it came time, we could put you in hospice at home for at least a couple of days. I wanted you to be able to sit in the sunroom a couple more times and enjoy the view.

The decline in the last few days went too rapidly. It was not possible to give you the couple of days at home, which is something that I grieve. The only moments of joy that we could give you those last few days was through relationship and touch. I wanted to give you more, but at least we could give you what was most meaningful.

Love,
Louis

Letter 29
A Letter to My Brother John

John,

When we were growing up, Mom worried about how we seemed to never get along. This is only a vague memory now. The conflicts and disagreements are hard to remember—not from fading memory but from a different relationship guiding which memories are more prominent.

In college, we discovered that we were more alike than we believed. When we were both Resident Assistants, at the beginning-of-year training all the RAs lined up in accordance with their Myers-Briggs scores. In three of the four domains—extraversion/introversion, sensing/intuition, thinking/feeling, and judging/perceiving—we were right next to each other. In the fourth, one person lined up between us. This perplexed both of us, but it also seemed to encourage us to explore our relationship and grow closer.

We maybe are not as similar as we once were and do not know each other as well as we once did. Our lives have grown busy, and we have pursued some different paths. We are still close but have not prioritized time together as much as in the past. While we both idolized our father in our youth, you have grown to be more like him while I have grown in different directions. There is still much that we share with Dad and each other, and our father played a significant role in that.

When you were inaugurated as president at Bemidji State, I was proud that Lakoda and I were able to be there. Mom and Dad, due to Dad's health, could not attend. It was important to be there in their stead, and it was important to be there as your brother. About two months before, I severely tore my calf muscle doing what could be described as typical Hoffman Brothers, Inc. behavior. While staying at an Airbnb in the Bahamas, my brother-in-law, Dee, and I decided we would help the owners and spray a large hornet nest under the deck. As I ran away, I felt a pop in my calf. Within a few minutes, it had swollen to nearly double its size. The ER doctor lectured me over and over, "You are over 40. You have to stretch before any exercise." I guess running from a hornet nest is exercise after 40.

The doctor's orders included 6 weeks with my leg elevated above my head for 20 hours a day. I am our father's son, so of course I did not follow the directions perfectly and returned to work before advised. Lakoda came with me for your installation as president as I was just off crutches, and it still hurt to walk. I worried about the trip given my calf, but it was too important to not be there. As we talked about this since Dad's death, I know it hurt that Dad never really experienced any of your presidency, making it even more important that Lakoda and I were there.

At the inauguration, it was evident that you already gained the respect of many at Bemidji State and were doing this right. This was no surprise to me. The most meaningful part of the trip, however, was the evening after the event. After some socializing at your house, several former students and mentees shared about the impact that you had on their life. In addition to being inspired by how you influenced them, I also saw many ways that you were like our father. I was very proud of my older brother.

From the first time either of our parents encountered health issues, one thing that I felt assured of is that we would not be divided. As a psychologist, I have heard many stories of families going through the death of a parent. Often, families are torn apart. I knew that would not be us. Even the assurance of this was a gift.

Our closeness over the years has made it even more meaningful to pass on the legacy of "The Hoffman Bros, Inc." to my sons. As of yet, they do not fully appreciate what this means, though I often have shared with them about how important our relationship has been as adults despite it often being rocky when growing up.

The shared grieving process has brought us closer again. When we were both at home together the first time after Dad's death, we had a couple of good conversations with many tears and memories, as well as talks of our dreams and future. Any distance that seemed to have grown faded away. Many rituals of grief can serve to help fill gaps in what is lost in our life, including our support system. While we were already in each other's support system, the grieving seems to be pulling us back to a closer place in it. I am thankful for it, and we are blessed.

We will always be bonded by many years of shared projects, support, laughter, and too many Hoffman Brothers, Inc. decisions. Those are best not for this book, but I am grateful for it all.

Love from your proud little bro,
Louis

Me, my junior year of high school, with my brother, his senior year

Letter 30
Bonus Family

Mike and Michelle,

The week of the funeral, I joked several times about how Dad, a conservative icon in one of the most conservative districts in Iowa, had such a nontraditional family. We are an international, biracial family. We are a family of different gender identities, different political affiliations, and different ideas of about faith and spirituality. Not all of us are a family through shared DNA or marriage vows, but that is not how we came to define family. While we have wandered through different paths, in the end, we were united despite our differences, and we did this during a time when the world around us is terribly divided.

When Dad's health was deteriorating, we played different roles. Michelle, you carried so much during this time, being the one who shared a zip code with our parents. Mike, you were a drivable distance, often able to be there more readily than John or I, especially in urgent times. I cannot imagine how Mom, John, and I would have made it through the last year without all of us coming together—biological and bonus family. I am better for the shared burdens.

As Dad's health deteriorated, we did not always agree, but this did not diminish the support we had for each other. This would not have happened if it were not for loving parents. Without them, we would have been classmates, acquaintances, or friends, but not family. It was a different path to becoming family, but I am thankful to our parents for loving and persevering.

The path was not always easy. There were adjustments that needed to be made, including when spouses and others joined the family. It took a few years to make sense of this very nontraditional family. During this, I am sure there were times when the bumps and adjustments were not always pleasant for you. These now have been resolved and are left to the past. I am sorry for my part in these and even more thankful that through the challenges of our father's deteriorating health we became even closer. From my vantage, the depth of family bonds strengthened through our father's final months and death.

When the time came for the obituary, the viewing, and the funeral, there was no doubt that we would be there as family, even if many who came to these rituals did not understand why. As Dad would say, we are blessed. And, I am blessed by having a bonus family.

Love and appreciation,
Louis

Family photo with all the children and grandchildren at my parents 50th wedding anniversary, December 28, 2018

Letter 31
Listening

Dad,

I have a vivid memory of watching you listening to someone. It is likely that the memory, despite its vividness, is more of a composite memory than a specific time you were listening. The background, your clothes, and everything but your face and body posture has faded from the memory. You were not looking directly at the person, but rather intently at some spot on the floor a short distance in front of you. But the intentness of your listening was clear. The earlier images of this composite must be from when I was young. The image became more crystallized as similar images combined with the earlier ones.

A central part of my job now is being a listener. I am often told by clients that they are impressed by my memory. I find this interesting, as I am often frustrated with what I forget. I want to remember every important thing my clients say, but I know this is not realistic. But I do listen intently.

As a therapist, I listen differently than you did. Many clients have told me something along the lines of "You stare a lot." I generally laugh and agree. I do. I often stare when people talk to me. My listening can be intense as I seek to take in all that I possibly can. It is easy for me to lose track of how intense this can be. It is different with telehealth sessions, where it is more difficult to take everything in when staring at the screen. With telehealth, I absorb more when I look away from the intensity of the light and allow myself to be more present through my peripheral vision. This is part of why I strongly prefer in-person therapy.

When with friends and family, I often listen better by assuming a posture like yours, where I am often looking off somewhat to the side, but intently listening. When clients read something, I listen better this way. I think about these different listening patterns and stances often, pondering what they mean and how they impact the people I am with.

There is a good friend of mine, Ed Mendelowitz, whom I have similarly appreciated watching listen. He listens differently than you, but there is something in the intentionally and intensity that reminds me of you. I once took a picture of him listening to someone in China. I could feel the intensity of his listening from across the room. I could feel the deep interest and caring without joining the conversation or moving closer.

Your intensity was qualitatively different than Ed's. There is something therapeutic that I sense with Ed. With yours, I felt the care but the curiosity was more intellectual, seeking an understanding in the service of a solution. Ed's was one that calls one to plumbing the depth of one's psyche, drawing them into the emotions and personal reflection.

Although I am a good listener, there is still something I can continue to learn from you and from Ed. After all these years, I am still developing the qualitative aspects of listening. My clients may owe you a debt of gratitude for what they benefit from the listening that I offer.

Now that you're gone, I am still attending to your listening and still learning from it. And I am still trying to listen to you.

Still listening,
Louis

Letter 32
Devlun

Devlun,

Reading your social media post after my father died, I know that you knew he was proud of you. That brought up strong emotions in me. I am thankful that you knew that he cared about you and was proud of you.

My father was always someone who enjoyed talking about the people I knew growing up. There were many people whom he was proud of, but there was something different—and special—in the pride he expressed for you. He knew your path was not easy, but you found a way to become a success and have had, it appears, a good life.

We have not seen each other in many years. There is a lot of life between the last time we were face to face. After I graduated college, I gradually left my connection to rural Iowa behind, even though it still had a special place in my heart. My life went in different directions that did not fit with rural Iowa. Being happy with this new life, I did not think too much of the friendships of my youth, with a few exceptions.

When we were growing up, there were periods where we hung out quite a bit. There was an appreciation for you, but, sadly, I do not remember those times well. I wish more memories from the period of my life remained with greater clarity. But when I distanced myself from Iowa, the memories also became more distant.

Several years ago, my father mentioned that he had connected with you. I believe it was shortly after you were elected mayor of Ida Grove. After that, rarely was there a visit to Iowa or one of his visits to Colorado where he did not mention you—in many phone calls, too. He loved success stories, and yours was particularly inspiring to him. While it had been many years since we had been in contact, I felt deeply proud of you as well. Some of that was from our friendship, and some was a sharing in my father's pride.

My father cared for, helped, and mentored many people. But his pride was not given out as easily as the other forms of concern. For him to be proud, there was generally a recognition of hard work, overcoming challenges, and being a good person who contributed to their community. Devlun, I hope that you will always carry with you the memory that my father, Clarence Hoffman, was very proud of you. He continued to speak of you through the last weeks of his life when many others of whom he often spoke were no longer prominent in his memory. This was a testament to how much you and your story meant to him. This pride in you also brought happiness and many smiles to my father.

Wishing you many blessings,
Louis

Letter 33
A Letter to My Sons

Lakoda, Lukaya, and Lyon,

There is a lesson that I hope you someday learn: the death of your father can break you, and with that it prompts reflections and lessons about yourself as a person and as a father. It is not that I want you to hurt or be broken. Rather, I hope that I was a worthy enough a father to be broken over. If I was a good enough father, my death someday will hurt and may even temporarily break you. That's the deal. But I hope the memories and knowing how deeply you were loved will give you treasures to take with you. I hope these will keep you connected to me when I can no longer be there for you. I hope they will outweigh the grief.

I do not know what happens after death, but I have little fear of being dead. There is a deep sadness and anxiety at being separated from you and other loved ones. In part, this is because I love life. There is so much to love being in this world, even in troubled times like what the world is facing now. Even amongst sadness, there is beauty in being there for each other in the pain. The deepest sadness in my own reflections on death is not being there for the people that I love, not being able to see how their life will go. As I accumulate more close connections with people younger than me, the sadness grows. I would love to see what happens in the lives of so many people, but their existence will extend beyond my years. Of these, not being there for you is my greatest sadness and my greatest fear.

Even knowing my life will have passed so that my eyes will not witness you being hurt and broken, the anticipatory sadness and empathy is alive within me now, hopefully several decades in advance. As your father, I have wanted to protect you from some pains; but more importantly I have wanted to be there for you through all of them. Being a White father of biracial children has impacted this. As a White male, I have seen behind a curtain that you will never see but will be impacted by. People, seeing my light skin and blonde (now graying) hair, have assumed it was okay to say things that are not okay to say to anyone.

This includes many "good people of the world" who profess being allies and others who are good at hiding their fear and hate. What I have borne witness to terrifies me.

I do not know where or when, but I know you will experience the deep wounds of racism. The years of being seen as different will wear on you. Though as a White father I can never fully understand your experience, there is nothing I want more than to be there for you when these wounds happen—protecting you when I can, comforting you when I cannot.

Being a father is something that I have reflected on deeply since Lakoda was born. Over the last four to six years, it has shifted to focus on comparing the father I have been to the father I wanted to be. I do not always fare well in these reflections. I have had many people tell me that it is obvious I have been a good father. At other times, people, such as clients, tell me that they imagine I must be a great father. My reaction to such statements is always mixed. I feel proud of you in these compliments to me, and they are nice to hear, especially when genuine. But it is also hard for me to hold them. I have not lived up to the standards I set for myself as a father. My hope is that maybe, like my father, I have been and will be a good enough father. In this, maybe I have sufficiently offered you the freedom to recognize and be honest about my limitations and failures. They were not failures of love, but they were my failures.

In wanting to prepare you for the world in which you have lived, your mother and I had to make difficult decisions. The most difficult decision, which is one faced by most parents of children of color, is when to take your innocence in the service of protecting you. My parents did not have to make this decision with me, or if they did it was in very different and less profound ways. You could not do things that I have done because it would be too dangerous. More tears have flowed from my eyes when facing this reality than I could conceivably count. When I see your anxieties, fears, and tentativeness, I often become overwhelmed with guilt and fear and anger—sometimes even rage.

Guilt is a close friend of mine, one that I generally appreciate. Guilt helps me be a better person. But this guilt is different and more burdensome than many other experiences of guilt. It is connected to a fear that I have failed you, maybe preparing you for possible dangers more than comforting you in the face of the realities of the world you have been thrown into. The deepest pain from the guilt comes when witnessing you struggling to be open with your emotions and struggling to connect in relationships. The depths of emotions and relationships are among my deepest values, and I worry I did not prepare you to embrace these, instead focusing too much on your physical and psychological protection from the world.

My fear and anger are connected to the world in which you must live. This is something that I could never quite help your grandfather understand. His optimism would not let him see the world honestly, and maybe I sometimes looked at it too honestly. I wanted him to know that the world would not always treat you right and any privileges he had passed to you through me would not be enough to protect you from the hurt the world will impose upon you. While everyone gets hurt, I wanted him to know that it would be different for you.

When you were young, when you stayed with your grandparents, I spoke with them about how they had to be aware they were taking care of biracial/Black children. I spoke with them about staying close in stores because people may be watching you more closely. I spoke with them about the danger of playing with toy guns, telling the story of Tamir Rice.[1] There were so many more things we discussed. As I shared this, I watched Grandma become sad. There was comfort in this because I knew she understood. But Grandpa struggled. Oh, he loved you so much. But maybe he loved you so much that it prevented him from seeing the world as it is. This is a luxury common to most White people that parents of children of color do not have.

The three of you are the most important people in my life. But I do not know that my choices always have reflected that. At times I worked harder at trying to prepare the world for you than preparing you for the world. I tried to fight, write, and teach about social justice. I tried to heal the world and challenge it to do better. Maybe I have made a small, small dent, but the hurt and hatred of the world has been on full display in the weeks that I have been writing these letters. Your history is censored for the comfort of White children and White people while knowledge of the history that could help protect you is being withheld. I have failed and was naive to think I could do more. This naïveté is part of my privilege, thinking that joining with others we could become powerful enough to overcome most of the racism of the world. Because I believed this, seeing what has happened since 2016 and more acutely

---

[1] Tamir Rice was a 12-year-old Black child who was killed by police when playing with a toy gun in a park. Observers call 911 reported a person with a gun in the park. The police aggressively drove onto the park grass, near the young child, shooting him and killing him within seconds of their arrival.

in the early months of 2025 have hurt and angered me more than many people of color who knew better than to get their hopes up.

Maybe I will have another 45 or so years to try to make up for these mistakes and to continue trying to change the world—hopefully with less naïveté. Much of my focus on being healthier is for you. And sometimes the excessive amount of work I do is connected to trying to make the world better for you. I get this from your grandfather in a way. He worked hard, in part, to give John and me, and later also Mike and Michelle, and all our families, a better life. For him, this was through earning a good income. I have not been as driven toward income—to a fault. But I have been driven to make the world a better place and to make people's lives better. While your grandfather and I had different paths and variations in our motivations, the result of being a workaholic was the same. While I have done better in recent years, I cannot justify my mistakes, even when made with good intentions. Living with the fear of not being good enough as a father will always haunt me.

I am sorry. I wonder about your reaction to reading this letter and how it will change over time. My worry is that your reactions may feel like a burden. My hope is that they are freeing and reflect the depth of my love in a new way. Some of the most freeing words that your grandfather spoke to me were ones giving me permission to recognize his imperfections. It took me years to accept his invitation. Maybe you can be wiser and accept my invitation earlier than I did his. Time will tell. It breaks my heart that I most likely will not live long enough to see your answers, as my father did not live long enough to see mine. Maybe, though, you can find ways to preserve the love and lessons after I am gone as I have with your grandfather.

I hope you will know that my love for you is a part of most of the successes and accomplishments of my life. If I was able to do my part in changing the world, you were part of this change. This love has never been far from my heart or mind.

With the deepest of love,
Your Papa

Part 5

Preserving Connection

Letter 34
Your Hands, Part I

Dad,

When I was young, I remember thinking about your hands, wondering how an insurance salesman had such big, strong hands. Surely it was not from circling your thumbs, as you often did when driving. Part must have been from growing up on the farm. Though you no longer did physical labor, it seemed your hands remained strong.

There was something comforting with your strong hands as a child. They helped me feel safe and secure. I loved watching you when you worked on the lawn mower. This was your strong hands in action.

As I grew into adulthood, I continued to notice your hands. I loved lifting weights and for many years pushed myself to where I had become quite strong. Though I cannot lift like I did in my youth, I still enjoy weightlifting. Yet, your hands seemed to me to remain bigger and stronger than my own. Maybe this is the father effect. Maybe my hands had grown bigger and stronger but somehow still seemed smaller and weaker than yours.

During your last several hours, your hands took on a different significance. Shortly after I arrived, I realized no one was touching you. This bothered me. Rationally, I know Mom had likely been holding your hands or touching you before everyone arrived. There was a flurry of activity when I came in—catching me up on where things were, checking with the doctors and nurses, talking with hospice, and greeting people as they came by. I also knew the others had been there longer, and I had just arrived. But I did not want your hands to be left untouched.

I took the chair by your bed and held your hand. Until I left to check on my class that was being taught remotely, I held your hands. I encouraged others, too, to hold your hands. At times, you would reach out with your other arm, and I encouraged someone to grab and hold your hand. Each time you grimaced, became restless, or appeared to struggle, I would gently stroke your hand or the side of your head. I did not want you to be alone. Even if you could not sense someone was present in any other ways, I was confident that the touch would let you know someone who loved you was there.

You were not big on touch, and we did not touch a lot. It was not that we were not close; it was just that in rural Iowa Germanic culture touch was not as common. Over time, being in the humanistic psychology world and having friends and family who engaged more with touch, I have become more comfortable with and enjoy touch.

After class, I had to purchase a suit jacket and something to eat. I was frustrated this took so long. I just wanted to get back to where you were. I returned to sit with Mom, Mike, Missy, and John on the other side of the room from you. You had been sleeping more restfully, so it seemed okay to be across the room. And it seemed more important to be there for Mom for a time. But around 9:00 PM, you become more restless again. I felt called to go back over, but it also seemed to disturb your sleep. I stayed across the room but felt somewhat tormented by that decision. I was drawn to touch.

A few hours later, you were gone. Shortly after you had died, I touched your leg. It was still warm, which provided some odd temporary comfort. Then, later, when we were leaving and had given the okay for the funeral home to come take you away, I touched your leg again. The warmth had faded and in sadness, I knew.

Love,
Louis

Letter 35
Always Enough

Dad,

There are a few stories our family loves to tell about you—and laugh. When told in your presence, you often would have a wry smile. One day when you were going to the store during the holidays, Mom asked you to pick up some pies. You returned with 13 pies! This was typical you. If you were sent to the store, we had to be specific with the product and how many to get. If we were not specific with the product, you would get a range of similar products to make sure that it included what was wanted. If we were not specific in number, you would always get more than needed.

Now I often do the same thing. If Heatherlyn does not tell me specifically what to get at the store, and I cannot reach her, I will get several options to make sure it was what she wants. When one time during the holidays she did the same with a list she took to the store, we teased her, saying that she was at last officially a Hoffman.

During some periods growing up when John and I were home alone more often, you talked Breadeaux Pizza into making pizzas that you could put in the freezer so they could always be ready when we wanted one. As we grew older, there was always enough pizza to throw one or more in the oven when friends were over. You also would invite our friends to just stop by and cook a pizza at times. More than once, I came home and one of our friends was there eating pizza without us.

You always wanted to make sure that there was enough. Some of this, I believe, was compensation. You took care of people. You always wanted to pay the bill at restaurants and treat others when you could. I remember one time after graduate school sneaking off to pay the check in advance to show you appreciation. It was quickly evident that it did not come across as I had hoped. You insisted to give me enough cash to cover the bill and more.

The compensation also seemed related to how much time you were away. John and I were latchkey children a good portion of growing up. Much of this was related to Mom's health and you working a lot. Vivid memories remain of being home alone in the evening, standing by the window, and watching for the headlights to start coming across the driveway. Although scared, I never wanted you or Mom to know this. Once I saw the headlights, I would scurry off to watch TV or to my room so that you would think everything had been okay. Still, you were aware that how much you worked was sometimes hard on us.

You carried a lot. The people who worked for you depended on you. Many community organizations depended on you. Your friends depended upon you. You set yourself up for this, and in many ways, I have replicated this, too. If I am honest, I still carry some resentment about how much others asked of you as an adult. But it is not the resentment one might expect. After listening to all the stories about you at the viewing and funeral, I am more appreciative than ever of what you did for others. I am okay with the costs that came with helping the people who showed you appreciation.

At the same time, there were people who took advantage of you. You gave them your time or helped them financially, but it was not appreciated. At the viewing and funeral, I could not help but notice some of them did not bother to attend. Maybe it was their own shame knowing this. Maybe they were dealing with things that I could never know. My resentment is not toward you or those who showed you the appreciation you deserved (even if you did not care if you received it); it is toward those who did not show you appreciation.

As I write this letter, I feel conflicted—more so than with any other letter. While the reasons for the behavior may be different, I am much like you. Sadly, I have developed similar habits and often struggle with guilt about having worked too much while my sons were growing up. I guess we are a classic "Cats in the Cradle" family.[1] Like you, I often give much to others. Also like you, I generally do not worry about the return. There are the times where I get frustrated, mostly when I have been making efforts in organizations without others also making the same investment or doing their part. This has decreased and has become rare with time, partially because I am with healthier organizations now. Well, they are healthier as far as the systems, but not always financially healthier. This "gift" is from you. The generativity mindset, or "heartset," is a gift.

I worry, Dad, about how you experienced this and if you continued to carry guilt similar to the guilt that I carry. These questions now can

---

[1] This refers to a song by Harry Chapman: Chapman, H., & Chapman, S. (1973/1974). Cats in the Cradle [Recorded by H. Chapman]. On *Verities & balderdash* [Album]. Elektra.

never be answered. But I want you to know that even when you were not perfect, you were always enough. You provided us with enough love, time, and support that John and I both grew up happy and successful. There have been things to work through, but even there you helped prepare the way.

While I have often said that my becoming a psychologist likely came more from similarities with Mom than you, there was a significant role you played as well. Some therapists may not appreciate me sharing this, but few people pursue a career as a counselor or psychotherapist without having faced their own challenges and suffering. I often have said, too, that I would never want to refer anyone to a therapist who has not experienced and engaged with their own pain and suffering, preferably at the depths. It does not need to be the same as what their clients experience, but the process of working through these struggles is important preparatory work for being a good therapist. You prepared me for being the person, therapist, and supervisor I am by modeling generativity and in giving permission to see you as imperfect. The help and support I have been able to offer clients, students, and supervisees has a lot to do with you and Mom. The opportunity to help others is maybe one of the greatest gifts you have helped me attain. There is something sacred in being a psychotherapist, educator, and mentor. Today, it feels important to share that credit.

I do not know with any certainty whether Heatherlyn, my sons, my friends and colleagues, my students, and my clients experience me as enough. I suspect the answer is not always what I would hope, especially because like you I too often take on too much. If I can be enough in any realm of life, I hope that it can be relationally—in my love and care for others, the diverse others who fill my life and bring me joy. This is my deepest and most imperfect pursuit in life.

Dad, thank you for being enough, and helping me to strive to be enough for others, too.

Gratefully,
Louis

Letter 36
Waiting for the Sunrise

Dad,

There are days that to wake up to sunshine, or even the sunrise, is too much. Maybe that is why, for much of the last year, I awake each morning at 4:00 AM. I want to sit with the darkness for a while, watching for that which is only illuminated within its presence. Then I wait for the sunlight to patiently emerge, preparing me for the light I know is inevitable. Today was such a day. I awoke a little before 3:30 AM. I did my morning routine of doing a couple of brain games to keep my mind strong, then read through the daily fact checks. I decided this morning to come to work early. It was dark, with no signs of the morning, when I left the house. One could not even see the traces of the mountains to the west.

On much of my drive today I had been softly crying, listening to my "existential reflections" playlist, thinking about you and thinking about the state of the world. Nearing the exit for my office, I was contemplating the pain of awareness and the comforts of self-deception. I have long been drawn to the former. The world is moving in what I fear is a dangerous direction. It seems that even many of those speaking out or even screaming do not see the depths of the risk. There is a deepening of polarization and, even more concerning, a growing tendency toward dehumanization. People speak to the specific issues without recognizing—and without feeling—the more profound risks. Political divide and dehumanization have always been with us, and sadly always have had a prominent place at the table. But there is something different in the dehumanization that we are seeing now. Even good people are being lulled into believing some of its lies. I am scared for my sons. I am scared for people I love and care about. I am scared for the world. Maybe it is good that your ability to stay aware of the world faded before having to witness this.

As I neared the parking lot, I noticed the first signs of the eastern sky preparing for the sunrise. It was not enough yet to even reveal the outline of the mountains standing in opposition on the other horizon.

The passionate dark purple touched up against lighter, sorrowful shades of blue. The clouds captured some dark grays to break up the colors. I felt inspiration in each. As I backed into my usual parking spot, I let the tears flow for a couple of minutes. I wondered how many tears called your name, how many stood as a testament to the sorrow of the world, and how many were my own sense of loneliness in the midst of all of this.

I stepped out of the truck into the cool morning. It is mid-March. The mornings have a comforting coolness as opposed to the starkness of a few weeks ago. Daylight savings started on Sunday, protecting more of the morning from premature light. From the front of our building, I could not get a good view of the sunlight creeping closer, and I felt called to it. I walked behind the building through some of the complex where it is located. For a few moments I took in the beauty. I found the parking lot lights a frustrating intrusion into the mixture of colors in the sky. I wish that I could see the beauty nature was revealing in its natural state. But I was able to set this aside to feel the beauty of the sky for a few moments. Then I returned to my office and began this letter.

Two weeks ago today, about 3:30 in the afternoon, I learned that you were at the ER. Within a few hours, I had spoken with Dr. Luft and was packing with urgency to get home while you were still here. As we left our home that evening, the darkness was overtaking the sky again providing some protection of darkness as we determinedly headed east into the night sky. The feeling of sadness was overtaken by the urgency of getting home in time to see you and be with you in those last hours. Watching the white lines pass by on the road, loneliness made its presence known, motivating me in the drive toward you.

Growing up, I loved the darkness. I liked my room dark, and I loved the night, often staying up into the early hours. This concerned you, and you told me that it was important to get more light. You loved the light and sought to allow as much light into the living spaces as possible. Through my college and graduate school years, I remained drawn to the night and its comforts. When writing papers, I often did not start until after 10 PM, sometimes midnight. I did my best writing then. During my postdoc, I transitioned to being a morning person. This was a surprise, but the tendency grew and now is firmly entrenched for many years.

Over the last 10 years, I have come to crave the light much like you. But there are times when I still prefer the comfort of the darkness. I need the balance of day and night, lightness and darkness. Or as O'Donohue stated, "We need a light that has retained its kinship with the darkness."[1] There are some things that can only be seen or found at night, or in what Bruce Springsteen titled in one of my favorite songs, "The Darkness on the Edge of Town."[2] I love these lessons. My ability to find precious things in the darkness and not fear the night is one of my most treasured talents. This has remained throughout my life, even as I have come to a place of craving the light. Now I sometimes crave the darkness just before the light instead of the darkness at the end of the day. It is not to force the light, but to let it emerge naturally, however long it takes, letting it gradually reveal itself without being thrust into the fullness of the light. I am still learning the lessons and significance of this change.

There is much about us in this, Dad. I do not know if you ever enjoyed the night. If so, I did not see it. You loved the light, much like you loved optimism. You had little tolerance for the negative, and you did not seem to understand how darkness could lead to a brighter, more authentic light.

You were the king of optimism. Even in your last days, in the midst of pain and suffering, you would force out, "I'm blessed, I'm blessed." You believed it at times because it was who you were, and you believed it at times because you forced yourself to or because it was the little bit of control you had left after so much was taken away by the cruelty of your fading health. When you forced yourself into optimism, I felt as far away as the western mountains from the eastern horizon. There was still ground that connected us, but it was so vast that it was impossible to see the path showing the way. At these times in the midst of your forced optimism, our conversations were lonely.

Dad, I wish we could have sat together in the darkness at times, intimately and genuinely connected. But this was terrain unfamiliar to you. If you went there, you shared it with few people. There were times when you would point to it from the distance, but you would never dwell in these spaces. I wondered if you, too, felt alone in these moments.

The last several years I have tried to explore the mysterious path from the eastern horizon to the western mountains. I have found pieces of the trails, but never the full path. I do not expect for the full trail to ever be revealed. It is a place where our relationship will remain a mystery.

---

[1] O'Donohue, J. (1998). *Anam cara: A Celtic book of wisdom* p. 4. Harper Collins.
[2] Springsteen, B. (1978). Darkness on the edge of town [Recorded by B. Springsteen]. On *Darkness on the edge of town* [Album]. Columbia.

Sitting in my office writing you this letter, I can see the mountains and a glimpse of Pikes Peak to the west. I watched the purple turn to blue and then to pink. Passion, sadness, love, and hope all reflected with vibrancy on the same mountains. Now, the light is starting to reveal their true colors as I finish writing.

I miss you, Dad, including the parts that you would never reveal. I wish that I could have known them—that you would have trusted me with them. I wish that I could have found a way to show you that these places are not so bad. I wish I could have chased these monsters away to allow you to be comfortable in the night. But I will have to settle for having arrived in time to hold your hand in those last moments. A darkness was coming that even you with your superpowers of optimism could not hold off. I could not hold it back either, but I could hold your hand and let you know through my touch, if not through words, that you were not alone. You were loved, and you were not alone.

Love,
Louis

The sunrise near my office the morning this letter was written

Letter 37
Nature, Bicycle Riding, and Grieving

Dad,

One of my favorite songs about loss is "Colorado" by Sons of the Desert.[1] I do not often listen to country music anymore, but there are some songs that still deeply resonate. "Colorado" is a song about the end of a romantic relationship, different than the grief I am going through as I write this. But there is a line that has come to me often over the years, and especially in the last weeks. It speaks of Colorado being too beautiful to be the place to get away from the pain and grieve. While this line has come to me often, it does not fit my experience.

Today, Lyon and I went for a bicycle ride. We have been riding a lot this past year and now we are preparing for RAGBRAI (the Register's Annual Great Bike Ride Across Iowa). I did not feel up for the ride, but I knew I needed it. It is just nine days since you died. I have not exercised since then, and I am feeling that. But I am also still feeling the lower energy. Conditioning wise, it was a tough ride. We only rode 14 miles with a little over 1,000 foot elevation gain—not much for us these days.

Once we reached the point of the ride where we were more in nature, I put on sad songs. I do not think Lyon knew it, but for much of the ride I was listening to sad songs and crying. There was something soothing and spiritual in the combination of nature, music, and the steady motion of the bicycle. I stopped to take a few pictures of nature along the way. Not many—I mostly just took in nature and the experience of awe.

A big part of my healing is feeling the different emotions concurrently. Feeling the freedom, awe, and joy alongside the grief was what I needed today.

Love,
Louis

---

[1] Womack, D. (1997). Colorado [Recorded by Sons of the Desert]. On *Whatever comes first* [Album]. Sony Legacy.

Letter 38
Genuineness and Kindness

Dad,

Since your death, I have reflected on kindness and genuineness often. While we both valued these, we were quite different in how they were embodied within us. You were more consistently kind, but my kindness is more consistently genuine. It was easy for you to have conversations with almost anyone. Growing up, John, Mom, and I often joked that we could not go anywhere without you meeting someone you knew. On vacations many states away from Iowa, you would meet someone you knew or a mutual connection. Soon after, you had a new friend.

As a small-town businessperson, building good relationships was important to your business; however, your kindness and friendliness were not just about business. It went deeper. In rural Iowa when I was growing up, it was common to wave when driving by other cars in town and often even on the highway. One day, you walked into our house and commented that someone did not wave back as you passed each other in your cars. You were concerned and wondered if you should stop by to check to see if they were doing okay. This is much more than your everyday kindness.

As a product of rural Iowa, I acclimated to these waiving rituals, but it was not natural. In part, this was due to my being shy and introverted. At college, there were several times when friends commented to me that I had walked by them on the sidewalk earlier that day without acknowledging them. Each time, this surprised me. I was deep in thought and did not notice people I know walking by me. While kindness is important to me, it is not the impulse that it was in you. I had to cultivate it from genuineness, empathy, and compassion while you went straight to kindness.

You were good at being kind with or without genuineness. This is not my strength. Genuineness has long been important to me, and I struggle when there is a lack of genuineness. The surface is not where I want to be, and I am not good at it. Recently, I have noticed my reaction when I have been called kind by several people whom I care about and respect. Their comments were genuine, but I found myself both appreciative and resistant. Reflecting on this, I view myself as compassionate, caring, empathetic, and even loving, but not always kind. On the surface, this seems paradoxical. This stayed with me unresolved for months leading up to your death.

At the viewing and funeral, many people referred to you as being kind. I trusted the people who called me kind, as I did the people who called you kind, but we were very different in this regard. The pull to resolve this mystery would not release me. I wanted it to connect us, and there are ways I want to grow in kindness to be more like you. Without a relationship and without genuineness I am not always kind. Even more, I am often unkind in response to a lack of genuineness.

When I started to move into professional leadership positions, it became common for people to try to "suck up" to me. Frequently this drew a quick ignition of anger inside of me. These disingenuous comments would cause me to not trust people and their intentions. This reaction is not great for someone in a leadership position, and I had to be aware and carefully monitor it. Most of the time, I was successful. In my last years of teaching, I cautioned students of a similar dynamic: writing what they thought I wanted to read in papers. This cannot be authentic scholarship or critical thinking, and it was very frustrating, even disrespectful, in my view.

So am I kind? Yes and no. The people whom I care about and respect who called me kind saw something in me that I could not. They were reflecting something deeper inside of me that I could not see. This pushed me to reflect more deeply on the genuineness connection. They were sincere in their comment, and they were right with their experience. It was not the whole picture but maybe a deeper part than what I was focusing on.

Clients have often told me that they imagine I never get angry or that I must be a great husband or father. These are genuine and relevant to the process of psychotherapy. I appreciate them, but deeper healing can occur with a human therapist than with an idealized or perfect therapist. They are genuine, but they are not the full story. I want to be human for my clients. I often respond to comments from clients that they cannot imagine me angry by saying, "My wife and sons can." At times, this seems to shock clients. I will offer examples, too. When customer service agents say, "I am sorry for . . ." or "that must be frustrating" and are obviously reading from a script, it takes great resistance, which I often do not have, to not get angry. In these moments, I am often not kind. Even with a few deep breaths, I am not good at faking kindness in these situations. You, on the other hand, were.

You were kind across relationships. For me, I am kind in relationships with depth and genuineness but can be unkind when these are lacking or when people are faking these. My goal is to be more like you while preserving my valuing of authenticity and genuineness. Part of my grieving is finding aspects of who you were that I want to incorporate into who I am. This struggle is not resolved. It is hard for me to be kind without trusting the genuineness or realness in the relationship.

You struggled with risking being seen as unkind when it was a risk worth taking, especially through avoiding conflict. When I was younger, so did I. Your context shaped this for you. Having spent your life living in smaller towns, and as a businessperson in smaller towns, your reputation was part of your financial security. Your conflict avoidance went beyond this, though. In part because of this, I witnessed little conflict resolution growing up. Mom pushed John and me to work through our disagreements, including making us stay in a room together until we resolved them and presented them to her. This was a great parenting technique, but I still was very conflict averse and lacking confidence to deal with conflict.

To be fair, you dealt with conflict that I never witnessed. You cannot run a business or be in politics without conflict. Now that you are gone, I regret not having witnessed you working through conflict or having talked with you more about how you dealt with it.

I pushed you to risk being seen as unkind. It was not a wish for you to be mean, but an encouragement to stand up for your family. Dad, I know you heard hurtful things about me marrying a Black woman, including from your colleagues in the legislature and people who voted for you. The position of influence you had may have impacted people. Yet, you were mostly silent, and your silence sometimes hurt. I wanted you to prioritize your grandchildren over being seen as kind.

I hope you note, Dad, that I have been talking about you not wanting to risk *being seen* as unkind. Confronting racism and microaggressions is not being unkind. But even if viewed as unkind, there are some behaviors that do not warrant or deserve a response of kindness. This does not necessitate being mean, cruel, or attacking; it just means that a response is warranted.

In graduate school, I learned that I could confront people and be good at it. When working in a psychiatric hospital, there was a colleague who had done something hurtful to me. I mulled on it for days, finally working up the courage to discuss this with my colleague. The result was a positive outcome and better relationship. Gradually, my conflict skills and courage improved. But it was not until entering into a biracial relationship that I really developed and utilized these skills regularly. My biracial family helped me recognize that ill-timed kindness can empower extremely unkind, hurtful, and even cruel, behaviors. I lost some kindness when I found my courage. It was a good trade, and the kindness remained in most of the right places.

Now I am trying to reconcile kindness, genuineness, and courage. This is one of your parting gifts, Dad. It is a way to keep you alive in me and let your kindness continue to benefit others. But I need to find a way to do this that does not sacrifice people I love and care about or my genuineness. I do not have the answers yet, but I am appreciative of this gift.

Love,
Louis

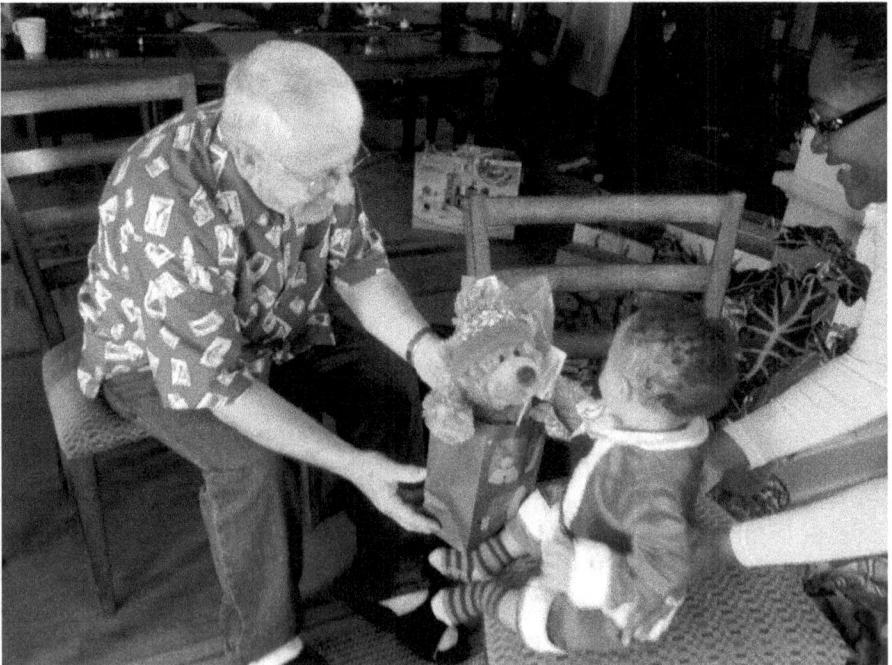

My father with my youngest son, Lyon.

Letter 39
Grief Bears Other Grief

Dad,

In my letters to you I have written often about the contingencies and connectednesses of grief and how grief prompts self-exploration. I awoke this morning to these weighing particularly heavy on me.

For several years, I went to a Jungian analyst and recently resumed seeing him. Although this has been broadly helpful, the dreamwork was particularly illuminating. My analyst helped me to clarify two dream symbols, Amaya and a friend whom I will call B. While sometimes people and pets may represent themselves in dreams, more often they serve a symbolic purpose. Amaya and B are very important to me, both having helped me through some very difficult times. In analysis, it became evident that Amaya and B emerged as symbols in my dreams when I was in need of comfort. With Amaya, this realization, along with a dream fragment, served as inspiration for my poem "A Visit."[1]

In this last month since you have been gone, I have wondered why Amaya and B have not visited.[2] There have been times I needed their comfort even when my eyes have closed, but they have not paid a visit that I am able to remember during sleeping hours. There is some comfort in knowing they likely have been there, just not remembered during the waking hours. Several times I have longed for Amaya.

We now have two dogs, Kalee, a terrier, and Aryia, who is a Siberian Husky, like Amaya. You tolerated our dogs, at best, because you knew they are important to us. Kalee is Heatherlyn's dog and makes that clear to everyone on a daily basis. Aryia is a great dog, but she is not Amaya. If Aryia was a therapist, she would be a play therapist. She comes to work with me sometimes, and lately there has been a strong desire to take her to work with me more often. She cannot come when I have in-person clients as she has a couple of bad habits that I have not been able

---

[1] Hoffman, L. (2016). A visit. In L Hoffman, M. Moats & T. Greening (Eds.). *Our last walk: Using poetry for grieving and remembering our pets.* University Professors Press.
[2] B has reached out offering support through messages, but has not emerged as a dream symbol.

to get her to break. However, she comes on days when my only in-person appointments are supervision. She makes sure I do not sit too much and loves when people come to visit. It is well beyond her comprehension that anyone would not love her and want to greet her.

Amaya, on the other hand, was more a therapist like I strive to be. She could comfort with presence, would stay very close whenever I was sad or struggling, and would cuddle with me. She was also mischievous, playful, protective, and loved to explore nature and the mountains. Amaya was a loyal pack animal, and I was her pack. These are qualities I have needed to be around me over the last month. I share many of these qualities, finding myself to often embody or seek to embody presence, protectiveness, a loving nature, and being a loyal friend. As maybe a smaller number of people see, I can also be quite playful and mischievous at times, despite my serious exterior.

Even just seeing Amaya in my dreams right now would help. I miss her more acutely now than I have in many years. Although I know better, sometimes there is some guilt with grief for Amaya coming up after your death. This is part of it. Your death is the most significant loss of my life, and the grief will likely re-emerge at any future deaths encountered in my life—as well as other events. It is just about a month until Lakoda graduates from high school. This is hard for me to believe, and I have been engaging in preparatory grieving about him leaving home for some time, most acutely since the first college visits with him. Mom will be here for his graduation, but you will not. It will be the first major family marker since your death. We will feel your absence and grieve.

Your death has prompted other symbolic and preparatory griefs as well. There are lost hopes and possibilities that have been the source of many tears these last few weeks. Most of these are relational as well, often connected to accepting limitations. Grieving you is enough. At times, there is resentfulness emerging that I must also engage these other griefs. Knowing this is part of the process frees me at times and constricts me at times. It frees me in knowing that it is not dishonoring you to give time to other griefs. The constriction is full of complexities and nuances that become both weighty and tiring. There are times I find myself wishing that I could just focus on grieving you.

I wish that I could talk with you about some of these issues. Yet, I know these are not the issues you were good with. You were always there and would listen, but some of the psychological complexities were too much for you. In business and politics, you could handle the complexities but not as much in the psychological domain. There is sadness in writing this. Maybe this is part of the origins of my often using verbal and written forms of processing, such as letters like these. When I was growing up, you were there and could offer advice at times, but you were not good at helping me ponder the psychological depths. If I discovered something in those depths when I was with you, it was through my own insights, with you providing the listening space. There is still power in this. With several clients I have worked with, the best therapy was mostly staying out of their way and letting them do their work in my presence. But, often, more is needed—presence, engagement, reflection, or other therapeutic processes. This is not a complaint, Dad. The space was appreciated, and generally I was able to do the work on my own. But there were times when I longed for something deeper in these conversations, too.

I have wondered what dream symbol you may become now that you are gone. There have been very few dreams in which you were present. But Amaya did not show up in my dreams until she had died, and B emerged in my dreams after a move where I did not see or interact with her as often, though she has remained one of my most treasured friendships. Maybe now you can find a new life in my dreams. I hope so. There is strong curiosity, and a little apprehension, thinking about what you may come to symbolize in my dreams. The complexities of our relationship suggest many possibilities. While the apprehension arises from an unlikely fear that you could be connected to some of the challenges I have written about in these letters, it is more likely that you will be preserved in my psyche with a more positive presence. I hope to see you in my dreams and find out soon.

Love,
Louis

Part 6

The Darkness

Letter 40
The Last Time I Left You

Dad,

I wanted to be there when you died. This was important to me, and I had given it much reflection. I knew there was no guarantee because we did not know when you would die. I had to plot estimates of when the time might come. I thought about this a fair amount in those last hours.

When my dog, Amaya, was euthanized, I was there. I stared into her eyes as she was given the shot, and she stared back at me. I remember watching how her eyes changed—the pupils, it seemed, collapsed while still in my gaze. It was both crushing and meaningful. In a poem written the night of her death I wrote,

> I stared into those blue eyes a last time
> I wouldn't look away
> So the face that loved you so deeply
> May journey with you from that last breath
> Then they were your eyes no more[1]

I knew your death would be different. While I loved Amaya, the relationship was not the same. And you were not being euthanized. I would not be looking into your eyes, seeing the moment of death reflected in the change of your eyes. But I wanted to be there. I wanted to somehow communicate that you were not alone. I wanted to savor the last moment of life and connection.

On February 27th, I originally planned to stay the night to be there with you and to keep Mom company. I was going to sleep there. Several family members discouraged this, so I said I would reconsider, especially as Mom urged this was not yet needed. But I stayed for a while, and I was prepared to stay the night.

---

[1] Hoffman, L. (2016). A visit. In L Hoffman, M. Moats & T. Greening (Eds.). *Our last walk: Using poetry for grieving and remembering our pets,* p. 154. University Professors Press.

At 9:00 PM, everyone else but Mom and I left. We spoke for a while, then she lay down on the bed they had brought for her and went to sleep. The nurse, O,[2] came to give you medicine at 9:30. I confirmed the medication routine for the evening. The priority was to keep you comfortable. You would get Ativan every hour and morphine every other hour. At 9:30, O told you she was giving you both medications. You said "okay," and swallowed as she gave you the syringe. That "okay" at 9:30 pm on February 28 was your last word.

At 10:30, O came back in. She told you she was going to give you medicine and tried to wake you, but you did not have any coherent consciousness left in you. I thought, "It is near." You could not swallow on your own. I remember being touched by how O gently stroked your throat to help you swallow. After she left, I went to sleep but awoke often, in part from the limitations of that brown chair in your room. Your sleep was restless; at times you coughed and other times you stopped breathing. This was the sleep apnea you had much of your life, worsened by being limited to your back.

At 11:30, O returned. It was the same routine, with her gently helping you swallow. You did not awaken or respond. At 12:30, I awoke a little before O returned. I tried to ascertain if your breathing had changed. You were not awakening, but I wondered if this could be because it was night. I assumed there was likely a day or two left. If you were going to make it through the night, I thought it better for me to go home and sleep so that the next night I could be there with you.

When O came in, the routine was the same. You did not awaken, and O gently helped you swallow. I asked her if she thought your breathing had changed. She did not think so. She asked if you had the sleep apnea for a long time, and I told her you had. Then she said that she has seen people not make it through the night in states like yours and others who had made it a couple of weeks. With this, she wrote my phone number on the whiteboard, and I decided to go home. I felt angst about this. My intuition, which so often I trust as a psychotherapist, was telling me to stay. Yet, my family encouraged me to go home, and O, while not pushing me one way or the other, indicated it could be longer until your death. I gambled. I told O how much I appreciated how gentle and caring she was with you and left.

---

[2] I am not sure the name of the nurse that evening, but I am deeply appreciative of her gentle and compassionate care, which seemed to be natural to her. I will refer to her as O.

That night, I walked slowly through the hospital. A fast, or even normal, pace did not feel right. Everything felt slow. I drove home slowly. Instead of going the faster route, I went through downtown Denison. It was quiet and lifeless, foreshadowing the coming hours. I arrived home and went to Mom's room to meet her new dog, Buddy. Sorry, Dad, but Mom used a compassionate lie and told you she was just dog sitting, but she needs Buddy, and Buddy needs her. I imagine a part of you knew this. But Joy was sleeping in your bed to keep Buddy company. He was still adjusting and did not like Mom being away.

I went up to get ready for bed. It was a bit after 1:00 AM when I laid down. I heard Buddy howl downstairs. There was something oddly comforting in the howl, and then I fell asleep.

Love,
Louis

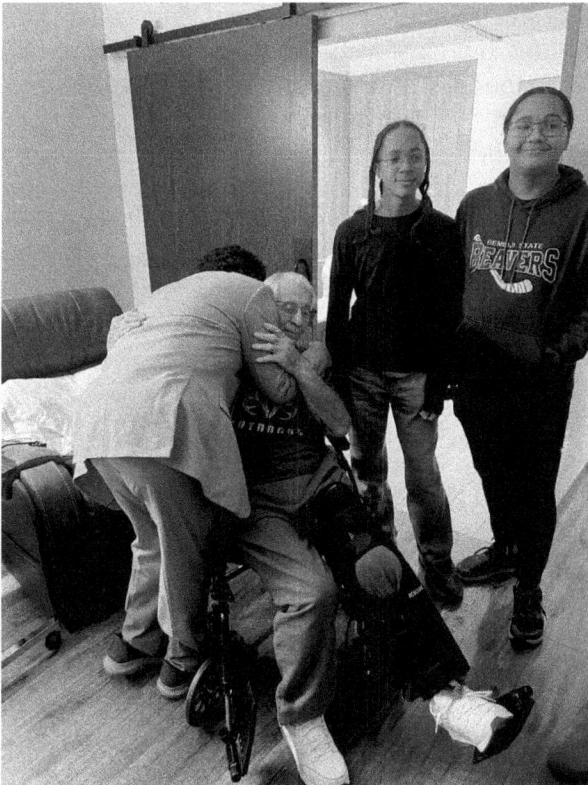

My sons saying goodbye to my father, Christmas 2024, a couple of months before his death

Letter 41
Guilt

Dad,

The morning you died I arrived home at 1:00 AM still wondering if I made the right decision to leave for some needed sleep. I was tired. We had pushed hard on our drive home. It was an emotional time, too. But being there was more important than rest or self-care.

Before I left the hospital, I asked your nurse, O, to call me if anything changed. She wrote my name and phone on the whiteboard in your room. I went to sleep thinking that I would get a call if Dad was likely to die that morning before I returned. A little before 4:00 AM, John knocked on our door. I did not register it in my deep sleep. Heatherlyn awoke, and then she awoke me. John came in and said that you had died. The guilt hit immediately, but I pushed it aside and responded to John. I told him I would get dressed and would be down in a couple minutes. As he closed the door, in frustrated tone I said, "I shouldn't have left."

Heatherlyn right away responded, saying, "Don't do that to yourself." I told her that I needed to feel the guilt so that I could feel the grief. As John and I drove to the hospital, I told him that, too. He also told me not to feel bad, and I told him that I needed this to move on to the grief. He then joked that I was a jerk for leaving. Though I did not laugh, I appreciated the humor and hoped he did not misinterpret my lack of laughter.

When we arrived at the hospital, Michelle was already there, sitting with Mom by Dad's bed. I went straight to Mom and gave her a long hug. We sat and talked. I apologized to her for not staying and for not hearing when she called. After this, I was able to go beyond the guilt. I am a guilt-prone person, and I am okay with this. I embrace this and feel no need to change. It is connected to many things that I appreciate about myself, so I will keep it and value this part of me. I can live with the guilt, but I cannot be me without the gifts I gain from this guilt.

Dad, I am sorry that I was not there that morning. I wanted to be. I tried to be there for your final moments. Though I have been able to shift my experience of this guilt, I know that I will have at least a twinge of regret and guilt for a long time, likely the rest of my life. I am okay with this, too. I know it is connected to my love for you, and the compassion that is part of who I am. I did not want you to be alone in those final moments; I did not want to turn away from your death. I wanted to hold your hand as your body gave way to release you from the pain and suffering you have been enduring.[1]

Love,
Louis

Christmas 2024, happy to be at home

---

[1] My mother later told me that O tearfully apologized for not being there when he died. While no apology was needed—she could not have known when he would die—this, again, showed her compassion and her heart. I am thankful she was the person taking care of him in those final hours.

Letter 42
Teaching Grief

Dad,

My life somehow became surrounded by grief. When I was growing up, there was approximately a 10-year period where in our small school, which averaged about 30 people or less per class, experienced a death. This included one close friend of mine, a teammate who was a year older than me, and another teammate who committed suicide. It was a lot of death for a small town of 500 people.

When building a client caseload during my Springfield years, somehow I started receiving many referrals for grief and complicated grief. Maybe people thought that being an existentialist made me an expert in grief. This work was rewarding for me, and ever since my caseload has often included a fair amount of people who are grieving. Later, people working in hospice sought me out for supervision. More grief work!

Mark Yang and I, along with a group of students, later traveled to several locations in China offering trainings on facing death—one's own death and the death of loved ones. We had many powerful and fascinating discussions as we invited people to share their experiences with grief and loss. A common theme was that the cultural rituals of grief were being replaced with more efficient ways of approaching funerals. As this change occurred, grieving became more difficult and complicated. This has happened in the United States, too.

Later I developed and taught courses on "The Use of Poetry with Death, Loss, and Life Transitions," and "Multicultural Perspectives on Death and Loss," as well as a course on Ernest Becker and Terror Management Theory (an approach that examines the impact of death anxiety and reminders of death). I also co-edited two poetry anthologies on death, loss, and poetry.

All this preparation for grief still cannot take away its sting. Each person must find their own way with grief, and it may not be the same across different losses. As I engaged the grieving process, there was a part of me that was curious about what path my grief would take. I had a sense about some aspects of grieving that would be important to me. Most of these intuitions were correct, but I appreciated the unique ways they played out for me. This reflects the commonly shared and individually subjective processes of grief. Despite all my knowledge about grief, I had to find my own path with it, even within the lessons known in advance.

When completing the book *Our Last Walk: Poetry for Grieving and Remembering Our Pets*, one of the co-editors, Tom Greening, found it very important to include "remembering" in the subtitle. The importance of this for Tom stood out to me and deepened my appreciation for the role it played in the grieving process.

While anticipating that remembering would be important, I was surprised with how it emerged. On the drive back to Iowa, the early letters I wrote sought to remember the process of the last day of your life. It was surprising to me that this was so important; there was a felt need to chronicle this before the memories faded. Over time, it became meaningful to record other memories, too, including some that faded until I was reminded of them in conversations with others. The memories of the last day, and the last months leading up to your death, were especially valuable to me and I want to stay connected with them.

At a conference in Europe, I had a lovely conversation with Edith Steffen, a colleague, about her research on "continuing bonds." This quickly resonated with me and with the "remembering" in the title of *Our Last Walk*. In many ways, this book of letters to you is an effort in continuing bonds—and it has worked. In it, my connection with you has both deepened and been preserved.

When developing the course "Multicultural Perspectives on Death and Loss," I watched documentaries and read many books on approaching death and loss in different cultures. I found this fascinating. Regardless of culture, rituals and community seemed to be central, even if these were quite different in the different cultures. I encourage clients to consider their family, regional, religious, and cultural rituals around grief. With your death, I was surprised with the rituals that were most meaningful and helpful.

One ritual that is newer is the slide show. This is increasingly common at funerals and memorials. Each family member found different pictures that were shared with the funeral home. They compiled them into a slide show. As the family sat near your body before the viewing, we laughed and connected as the pictures flashed upon the screen. It prepared us for the next three hours of greeting people as they came through the viewing.

Before the funeral, we were each given our last moments with my father's body. My mother went last. Watching her one last time with my father's body brought a flood of emotions. While the funeral ritual was not as central to my grieving process, it was for my mother and others. The internment was surprisingly meaningful. As my father served in the army, it was a military burial. As the shots were fired and the flag was folded and handed to my mother, I was deeply moved. I am thankful that my sister-in-law, Joy, snapped a picture right as Mom was given the flag.

The community at the funeral was not my community. Most of the people I did not know or did not remember. Yet, as I reconnected with several people who were important to me, the fragments of community left in Iowa brought some comfort. My community embraced me at a distance through emails, text messages, and social media. I felt their presence and love for me. The surprise here was how meaningful it was to see your community come out for you. While not my community, I was still a recipient of healing through your community.

I wonder how different the grieving process would be for me without my history of teaching and working with grief. This knowledge and experience could not protect me from the blow of your death, but it helped me savor the experience and meaning of the grieving process.

Love,
Louis

Letter 43
A Letter to Those Who Have Shown Me Compassion and Love

This letter is to more people than I could remember or name.

Grief calls us to community, and community can be a form of salvation. It was for me. During the drive to Iowa, I was cognizant that outside of family I had little community there. While I have many great memories from growing up in rural Western Iowa, it has not been my home for many years. As a biracial family it has become clear that it could never be home to my family. Preparing for my father's viewing and funeral, my sense of alienation was palpable. There were people important to me growing up that I was happy to see, and it reconnected me with an appreciation for the role they played in my life, particularly Sam and Gary. Despite these connections, outside of family rural Iowa tends to bring more alienation than comfort. Due to this, there was apprehension in putting so many miles between myself and my support system.

The label of introvert has often been applied to me, including by myself. This label is used variably and often too loosely. Contrary to many portrayals, introverts can be highly relational people as I am. While large groups and parties can be very draining, I love settings that foster building deep relationships. In the one-to-one, I am often energized as much or more than being alone, whether this space is filled with words or simply the silent presence of another person with whom I have a close connection. It is even easy for me to lose a sense of time in one-to-one conversations with people important to me. I have been blessed to have been able to help build an ideal work setting for me at the Rocky Mountain Humanistic Counseling and Psychological Association. We have our own building with a small training clinic, a few renters, and offices of a few close friends/colleagues. We are developing a strong community, but the foundation is building close, supportive personal relationships that the community is centered around. This community is my new bonus family.

Being more introverted, I often think of myself as close to a small number of people. However, gradually it is becoming apparent that this is not true. It would be more accurate to say that I am selective about the relationships in which I choose to deeply invest. It can be a bit overwhelming for me to think about the number of people whom I have invested in and developed close relationships with. Many of these individuals I may not be in regular contact with anymore while with others we communicate most weeks. I need my alone time and my relational time. This is similar to the paradox of "being a part of/being apart from" that Jim Bugental, one of my mentors, wrote and taught about.[1] This paradox is one that I experience intensely. I value both and thrive when they are distributed well.

John O'Donohue, in his book *Anam Cara*,[2] maintained that solitude is an essential part of relationship. This deeply resonates with me. When I have successfully cultivated and maintained deep relationships, the felt connection often remains when apart. Maybe this is part of how I am maintaining the connection with my father even when he is gone. My alone time is both intrapersonally and interpersonally relevant. I am able to be deeply with myself (i.e., intrapersonal) and at the same time feel how this is connected to my relationships with others (i.e., interpersonal). Because of this, I do not often feel alone, and when I do I recognize that it is important to listen. Typically, loneliness now emerges in the context of a relationship in which some alienation or unexpected distance has inserted itself, even if temporarily.

Since my father's death, several acute experiences have resulted from a combination of alienation, loneliness, and existential isolation. The specifics of these are not as relevant to this letter as the recognition of different flavors of feeling painfully and sometimes anxiously alone. This is a rare experience for me and has been juxtaposed with feelings of profound connection in a few new, as well as a couple of established, relationships. While some relationships, including important relationships I routinely rely upon, have felt more distant since my father's death, overall I have felt more depth and intimacy in relationships since he has died than I have felt in a while. The painfully alone and joyously connected are closely intertwined. They always are, but more intensely so in this season.

The community that stepped up for me at times surprised me. In many text messages and emails, I felt held in love and care across the

---

[1] Bugental, J. F. T. (1999). *Psychotherapy isn't what you think*. Zeig, Tucker.
[2] O'Donohue, J. (1998). *Anam cara: A Celtic book of wisdom*. Harper Collins.

miles. The process junkie in me was intensely curious about the felt depth of connection in these messages. In many ways, the surprises were among the most meaningful. On the day before my father's death and several days afterward, a number of messages brought me to joyous tears that freely mixed with the tears of grief.

My closest friend, Nathaniel Granger, Jr., is fond of saying, "I love love." In these moments of connection across the distance, I felt this deeply. Generally, I am better at giving love than receiving it—to the degree that I worry sometimes people may feel shunned when offering me support or love. I want to get better at this and hopefully am making progress. My father's death moved me along in this journey.

There has been a growth spurt in me since my father's death that is relationally based. Although I recognize my propensity for growth spurts during such periods of suffering, they do not occur without the fertile soil of a relational foundation. Part of me wants to name the many people who have been part of this to show my appreciation and acknowledge their role in this growth spurt, or even just name a few key people. However, there are too many names and too great a chance one would be missed and someone offended. It may be more meaningful, too, to share this in-person at the right time.

For those who reached out with love and compassion, or even sent it to me without words, thank you. This was not only appreciated and needed, but in ways it became transformative. I could write for another 50 pages trying to convey the depth of feeling this brings up in me, but I know the words would fail and fall short. So, I simply say the far insufficient words of "thank you."

With love and appreciation,
Louis

Letter 44
I Need to Feel Small

Dad,

It was three weeks ago today where I held your hand just a few hours before you left us in the middle of the night, and today I feel a need to be somewhere where I feel small. Ernest Becker wrote, "Man cannot endure his own littleness unless he can translate it into meaningfulness on the largest possible level."[1] I have always resonated with this quote, but today the intensity is more acute as I am called to embody it in a deeper way. I want to sit somewhere in the mountains where, on one side, I see the peaks sprawling above me, and on the other side, I see the city in the far distance. Most important, this needs to be a place where I am not disturbed by other people. I am just existing between the enormity of nature and populations of people going about their lives—both completely unaware of the pain and isolation that is permeating this day. Whether I look to nature or people, a sense of smallness infuses my existence. Today, I am living in a space that no one else can inhabit.

In a few hours, my first client will walk into my office. Once they arrive, I am confident that I will be able to be with them deeply and genuinely, offering them what they need. In doing so, I will not be able to be with myself for that hour, nor the next, or the one after. I love the work that I do, and I am thankful to be able to move between these spaces, even when feeling the strong call of the mountains this morning.

The last week has been a penetrating time of grief where the many contingencies of grief came to the fore in their own ways. The varieties of the grief process were, at times, beautiful, and at other times crushing. Much was about the loss of you. It was also about how the world changed without you being in it. Relationships and experiences also changed because my place in the world is not the same. The loss of you has impacted most of my relationships, though typically indirectly.

---

[1] Becker, E. (1973). *The denial of death*, p. 196. Free Press.

A week ago today I flew out to the Society for Humanistic Psychology Conference. Lakoda went with me and afterward we went to New York to visit a college he is considering. The conference was wonderful. I was often joyful, feeling deeply connected with people, and I was also feeling broken. Although I know there were glimpses of the brokenness that some of my more intuitive friends might have been able to catch, I was mostly able to remain hidden when the brokenness stepped forward, often suddenly.

At other times, I revealed myself—but never the full vulnerability. I found spaces where I could speak to the hurt of the world and my despair for the future, including when presenting. This despair is rooted in a fear that our country may be going in a dangerous direction while banality of evil surrounds us, empowering the dangers through complicity. In moments where hope could be touched, the community of other humanistic psychologists was palpably present. These moments of vulnerability and openness were real and powerfully felt. They were me, and the me I wanted to be. Yet not far away was another part of me that I wanted to find space for but could not. After the trip, a recognition emerged that when this other part of me beckoned, though it helped me feel more present intrapersonally, my attunement to others was not as sharp as usual. I grieved and felt guilt for what I missed, for not being as present to others.

For much of my life, I have loved the paradoxes and complexities. And there is part of me that loved this one, but another part of me wanted to escape. There were a couple of times where, in relationship, I felt drawn to be more vulnerable with people who had offered a space. But this was not the time, place, or context. During the last day of the conference, I often felt intense anxiety, which is not common for me. My comfort came in a confidence that it would go away once the plane landed in New York. And, for the most part, it did.

Our flight was delayed, then delayed again, then moved up before one more delay. In the midst of this fluidity, I wrote more of these letters. When we landed in New York, my brother-in-law, Dee, picked us up and we were able to stay with him. It was good to see him. I am blessed with great in-laws and thankful for this time. I was surprised, Dad, how much you came up in different ways while in New Jersey and New York. It was easy to step back and observe this as part of the grieving process while also being in it. There was a stark contrast from the first half of the trip, where there were many people around whom I love and are good friends, but too many to have space. This was part of the anxiety I felt in Atlanta.

Dee lives in Asbury Park, New Jersey. This is a place that Bruce Springsteen spoke and wrote about often. Growing up a Springsteen fan, and remaining one today, this was a very full experience. Springsteen wrote often about fathers and sons. While his relationship with his dad was very different than mine, I still learned much from Bruce about these relationships. I thought often of his comment at a concert I attended about being startled by the humanity of his parents. This I have always resonated with and wrote about in other letters. Once again, Bruce somehow helped me explore and process things that needed exploration.

The visit to the colleges was meaningful. I have worried about Lakoda attending these colleges because of the price and the distance from us. I was more impressed with them than expected but still worry. It was good to spend this time with him. There are reams of sadness about him going off to college. I am not ready for it yet, even if he is. This is another challenge I must face directly so that I can be the father he needs as he prepares for this transition. I do not know if this was a struggle you had back when John and I were leaving for college. We never had that conversation. You likely would not have risked intruding on what you viewed as our time.

Last night, Lakoda and I arrived home. While I enjoyed the trip and part of me wanted to keep taking it in, there was a need to be home. At first, I could not place this need. But this morning, the recognition emerged that it is a call to the mountains. It is a call to be where I can feel my smallness. There are times when it is good to feel insignificant. I want to see that the mountains will stand and the crowds will go on, even if I need to withdraw and grieve for a while. I need to know that beauty still exists now that you are gone. I need to know that I can be alone in the midst of all of this and be okay. I need the mountains.

Returning to the Becker quote, I know the meaningfulness to which my smallness is connected: relationships and making a positive impact on the world. But I am also learning a lesson today sitting in my smallness—one that I need to explore more in the mountains later today. I spend a lot of time focusing on relationships that are primarily for others. I have the relationships that are for me, too. But I do not always embrace these. I stand on my own too often. The profundity of the meaning of being in relational depth sustains me even when it is primarily focused on others. I love these spaces. But it is time I recognize that I need to accept more of the places where the relational depth is receiving as well as giving—where there is mutuality.

I see you in this struggle. You never let people be there for you. You were the mountain for many others. But you rarely allowed yourself to be vulnerable. This is one place where I tried to be different from you, but did not always succeed. I wish you would have allowed me to be there for you, to be a mountain. I know this is complex given you were my father, and I was your son. But I would have liked to know these spaces.

My life has been blessed with many good friends, including several whom I allow myself to be vulnerable with. I am glad that I have been able to be more vulnerable with my sons as they have grown, trying to find that developmental appropriateness and when to introduce this. It is a source of pride that I am able to be there for many others, too. Yet, I need to acknowledge my needs more often. Hopefully this can occur without sacrificing time for others. This grieving is providing an opportunity.

Tonight, after work, I will tell Heatherlyn that I might be home a bit later. I am going to take a drive to the mountains. I am going to let my smallness wash over me and invite rejuvenating tears to come.

Love,
Louis

The view from Gold Camp Road, Colorado Springs, the evening this letter was written

Letter 45
Coffee with a Friend

Dad,

I met with a good friend, Jason Dias, for coffee today. I arrived before him and pulled out my iPad, creating a blank note, then waited for him. After we ordered our coffee and sat down, I told him, "I may cry today. I have been doing that often lately. And I may take notes as I do. I do not want to lose any nuggets of wisdom in the sadness."

Jason, who has always been a wise soul, even back when he was a student, immediately understood and appreciated this. He shared a story about a mutual friend, Dave, who was a colleague of mine while I was teaching in graduate school and Jason was a student in our classes. Dave was very open with his tears, even when teaching, and it was beautiful. Sharing this remembrance was good timing for my grieving.

This provoked of one of my favorite stories of Jim Bugental. Jim is a famous psychologist and one of the early founders of existential–humanistic therapy. I had the privilege of training under him late in his life. By this time, Jim had sustained a stroke that severely impacted his memory. Depending upon the day, he could remember somewhere between 15 and 40 minutes. He would do therapy demonstrations that lasted longer than his memory that were quite amazing, illustrating the power of being in the here-and-now moment.

One day, there were about 30–40 students in a room with Jim. He had never met most of these students before, and most of whom he had met he likely could not remember. He told a simple but profound little joke, "I have spent all my life talking about the here-and-now, and now this is all that I have left." After he said this, he laughed a beautiful, authentic, free laugh. Then, very suddenly, he shifted to freely crying. The crying was just as authentic and open as the laughter. After he was done crying, he calmly said, "I am okay now. We can go on."

This experience was deeply moving. Jim was so open and without any trace of shame about the laugher and the crying. He was comfortable and open in his expression of both and did not try to hold them back; nor did he feel the need to explain or justify them. He was just with them. I am not, as of yet, able to do this so freely. It is easier for me to be free with sentimental tears than the tears of anguish that Jim shared so freely. There is a draw to the deep freedom Jim modeled; even in imagining it, there is relaxation that comes across my torso spreading to the rest of my body. I am not there yet but on the path and hope to get there. Of course, context and timing are relevant. Jim would not approve of being this free with his emotions in all contexts and settings, but even in his compromised state he knew where he was and that it was okay.

In your latter years, tears of sentimentality were often present in your eyes, Dad. These were beautiful, treasured tears that beckoned feelings of closeness. While your tears of anguish were rarely seen, the sentimental years revealed some of your heart.

The last few weeks I have felt closer to where I hope to be with my emotions. It has not been from being overwhelmed, as one might suspect after the death of a parent. It is from someplace deeper—someplace that feels purer. The process of saying goodbye to you has offered me this gift. I will take it and treasure it, even if sometimes it temporarily slips away.

Love,
Louis

Letter 46
A Return to the Depths

Dad,

Grieving thrusts us into reflection, whether ready or not. Though it does not outweigh the pain of the loss, I treasure the gifts that emerge from the reflection. When starting to write these letters, curiosity was a welcome companion alongside the grief. Previous experiences have taught me that curiosity would aid the grieving process and illuminate the trail to these gifts. Some of these gifts I resisted, or said, "Not yet." Others, even if resisted, would overcome my refusal.

Grieving you has brought more reflection than prior losses. Journeying into these letters—and other letters and journal entries that I decided not to include—revealed many gifts. The one most treasured is a return to the depths. In other letters, I have written about my lifelong pursuit of the depths, both the intrapersonal and interpersonal depths. For over 20 years, relational depth has been my most profound treasure—my centered space. Yet, over the last 10 years there have been times that, in retrospect, I lost this center and, in doing so, was estranged or alienated from myself. The value remained but my embodiment of it wavered.

In the last several years, even poetry has eluded me. Poetry has been a companion of mine since a little before my divorce, and it played a primary role in moving through the grief of that relationship ending. When trying to write poetry lately, it almost always failed. The words were flat and felt forced, even when the emotion was there. I could not channel it into creativity. For a couple of years as I knew your death was approaching, I thought maybe when you died it would revive poetry in my life. Instead, it brought the gift of these letters. Maybe the poetry will come later. I hope so. But I know the depths are already returning.

Since you have been gone, just existing in the world brought a rawness of being. At times, I could hide this away, but mostly I chose not to. Vulnerability and tenderness with myself have always lined the path to the depths. Like the early spring blossoms in Colorado, the depths are starting to emerge. It does not always feel good, but even when it does not, I feel blessed.

There is a quote that I have been trying to find for years. I am sure that it has evolved in my memory and is no longer fully accurate. I thought it was from Henri Nouwen, but I cannot find it in his books. The quote is along the lines of, "One cannot go into the depths of their pain without faith that there is something better on the other side." Maybe the calling to the depths is a profound trust that it will bring me to a better place—a better me.

An aspect of being an existential–humanistic psychotherapist that I value is the continual calling to self-exploration. In existential–humanistic therapy, the person of the psychotherapist is a primary component of psychotherapy. If we are not working on ourselves, we will not be able to help others. Often, we can do some of our best psychotherapy when we are vulnerable ourselves.

During my internship, a colleague made an error that could have been costly. Immediately, they were aware of it. They went to one of the supervisors, acknowledged the error, and suggested it may be best to go home because of being distraught. The supervisor listened, then warmly responded, "Or maybe you will do your best therapy tonight." My colleague decided to stay. In a meeting the next day, they tearfully thanked the supervisor and acknowledged that they had, indeed, done some of the best therapy they felt they had ever done. Sometimes there is opportunity when we are thrown into vulnerable spaces.

There are different genres to relational depth. In all of them, there is always a "profound contact and engagement" between individuals that includes realness, empathy, affirmation, presence, openness, kindness, and mutuality.[1] As a therapist, I seek relational depth with all clients with whom I work. Yet, there are some slight differences with how this is experienced and sought outside of therapy. While I am open to being deeply impacted, and even changed, in my encounters with clients (and often have been), there are subtle and sometimes necessary or required differences.

The relational depth I seek in my personal life is one where both of us are open to being touched and touching the other at the soul level; there is an openness to being deeply changed through encounter. The vulnerability and openness must be mutual, even if evolving and not always equivalent. The concern for and attentiveness to the whole

---

[1] Mearns, D., & Cooper, M. (2018). *Working at relational depth in counselling and psychotherapy* (2nd ed., p. 44). Sage.

being of the other person is imperative. While I pride myself on relational depth, I am more select with whom I engage this type of depth where I am not just open and vulnerable with who I am, but with who I am allowing myself to become through the relational encounter. The trust in the other person is not just at the behavioral level where failures and disappointments are inevitable; it is a trust at a soul level. Typically, when this level of trust becomes present, it is something I recognize early in a relationship at an intuitive level.

Earlier in life, I did not always trust my intuition about the trust toward relational depth. As I reflect on my life now, it is difficult to identify instances where this intuition toward accepting one into relational depth was wrong. There have been a few times where I was surprised by not recognizing the potential early but rarely has someone proven unworthy when a strong intuitive sense was present. What has changed is my refinement of and trust in the intuition from years of deep connection and relational wounds.

Now the beauty of the depths is calling me home. It is where I want to live, where I want to practice, where I want to be. But maybe this is not even the right metaphor because the depths are within me and have been all along. While we had a good relationship, Dad, I would not characterize it as one of mutual relational depth despite containing many of its qualities. I wanted that and sought it, but it was not who you were when you were alive in the flesh. I feel it with you now.

My temptation is to say that it is too late, but this does not resonate in my soul. It emerged when it was able. While I desired it when you were in the living years, if it must be now, I will take it. It feels that the barriers for us both have come down. My barriers were rooted in a fear that if I were to pursue this, I would fail. This is a failure of which we would share responsibility—it is not just you. In the living years, there was not the trust in something on the other side. Now, I have found the faith and vulnerability that I need to have this depth with you.

As my connection with you grows deeper, connections with others are growing deeper as well. As spring nears in Colorado, I see a new springtime in my life and relationships, too. There is blossoming all around. I want to take it all in. Dad, maybe it was not the way or time I wanted to find this, but I will not lament. I will be grateful that, in this "I am blessed."

Love,
Louis

Part 7

A Lifetime of Grief

Letter 47
Feeling Closer

Dad,

One of the surprises of the grieving process for me has been feeling closer to you than I have in a couple of years. Henri Nouwen wrote, "When you have loved deeply, that love can grow even stronger after the death of the person you love."[1] Aspects of this were easy to reconcile. The last several years there was less of you due to your dementia. Many of the changes were aspects of you that most people, including your friends, would not see. They were the softer edges of your decline that, paradoxically, exposed the harder edges.

You regressed in ways that made it harder to see how the realities of the world impact my family. They exposed some of the work left undone with your implicit racism, and some places where you slid back from some of your awarenesses and growth. Watching aspects of your decline, I first was able to accept that you were no longer able to learn and grow in some areas of your understanding of racial issues. After watching you face so much, this was difficult to witness. It was more difficult for my family to accept this, as they did not know your trajectory of growth as intimately. Later, I had to accept that you were also pulled backward.

The most difficult was when you were no longer able to see how some politicians you supported were doing things that directly hurt my family. Some of these same people are the ones who never sent a card or acknowledgment after you died. Some of these politicians asked for money and spoke highly of you while alive. However, I guess you were no longer of use to them when you could no longer write a check or speak on their behalf. I did not expect any more from these politicians, some of whom rose to high ranks of political leadership and elected positions. However, even when it was no longer fair, I expected more of

---

[1] Nouwen, H. (1996). *The inner voice of love: A journey through anguish to freedom*, p. 71. *Image.*

you. I wanted you to stand up to them. I wanted you to stand up for my family.

A few years before, we had some difficult conversations about White privilege, racism in politics, racism on some of the news channels you watched, and some things you "liked" or reposted on Facebook. You listened and even began to change some of your views as you saw the implications. But then came the time where you would listen and understand but forget by the next conversation.

I felt caught between the changes in you and my family. And Dad, I did not always manage these well. My priorities were standing up for my family first. Some of them were hurt by things connected to your regression and lapses, and they needed to know that I recognized this hurt. I recognized, too, that this was not you—and not the you that you were becoming. We all will reach a time when our growth cannot proceed as it did in our youth and even in our middle ages. I did not know how to navigate this and, at times, may have been too hard on you.

These dynamics were a painful reality in the latter years of your life. I often spoke about them with a few close friends, especially my closest friend, Nathaniel. Not all these friends could really understand, even if they tried. But Nathaniel seemed to be able to stay present with these and hear on a deeper level. I appreciated this. If not for Nathaniel, it would have taken longer for the barriers to start to fade. His friendship helped our relationship.

Over the last year, as your dementia took a deeper hold, I could feel the barriers begin to gradually fade away and the closeness return. It was a start, but it did not reach completion while you were still alive. For the last few years—aware of this process—I feared that you would die before the closeness returned.

The last Christmas helped. In the weeks approaching Christmas, you had started to struggle more in the evenings. You were frustrated that you were in a nursing home and could not go home. This is understandable. I would have the same frustrations. However, the anger became directed at Mom, who did not deserve this. I knew that you, at your best, would not say these things that hurt Mom. During the days, you did not. But as night came and Mom went home to avoid driving after dark, you were left alone. As I wrote in other letters, I volunteered to be a shield for Mom. Many nights we had conversations and your anger at her would fade—the monsters would go away. But I knew these were not conversations with "you." By the end, as your anger faded, glimpses of you re-emerged, but it was not you.

At Christmas, when we were all home, the anger at night was not there because each night someone was with you. We also were able to bring you home for part of two days. I remember you saying several times with happy tears, "This is so nice." You were so happy and seeing this was joyful. This was you. Each time your tears of joy came out so did mine. Then, each day when you had to go back to the nursing home, other tears replaced them. This first night, it was earlier than I anticipated. I rushed to get my family ready to head to the nursing home. The thought of you going from that joyous time at home to the lonely nursing home room at Christmas by yourself was too much. This was too big of a monster, and I needed to be there to chase it away. I wanted to be there when you arrived. While we did not succeed, we were there shortly after, and I did not see any monsters after we arrived. At the nursing home, there was not a lot of conversation with you. Our family spoke, and at times laughed and joked. I knew you could not always follow the conversation, but it was also evident that our presence was a comfort. In that silence, the closeness was there.

Gratefully,
Louis

Letter 48
Preparing for More Grieving

Dad,

The past two years has been a time with a lot of grieving. Several close friends, as I wrote in a previous letter, died in the last two years. While a couple of these were expected, most of these were people dying that I anticipated would be around for years, even decades, to come.

I have been blessed with many friends. As a shy, introverted child, much of my life, I would not have believed it if someone told me I would have as many good friends as are in my life. The age range of close friends spans at least a 50-year gap, with some friends being much younger, most being older. When I was living in Springfield, my two closest friends were a year younger and over 50 years older than I was. This was a strange and beautiful experience.

Robert Murney, who had been my supervisor and mentor, became a close friend quickly after I graduated. What started off as a mentoring relationship transitioned into a close, intimate friendship. When his wife became ill, one other friend and I were the two people he turned to. He also spoke openly about his approaching death, mistakes he made as clinic director, and his spirituality. We discussed our friendship, including him sharing with me that I had become a close friend. I treasured this but have rarely spoken about it before. There was something that felt arrogant about calling Murney a close friend when I was so much younger and less wise than he was. Many years after his death I am learning to claim this as something beautiful.

Murney recommended a book to me that I read several times: *Anam Cara* by John O'Donohue.[1] Aman Cara translates to "soul friend"—a friendship that goes beyond and is deeper than a typical friendship. After I read the book, we spoke of this often and the lessons for friendship. When I accepted a job in another state, he shared his sadness about me leaving as well as his happiness for me. I wrote him a poem (not a good one) that I framed and gave to him with a photo of us

---

[1] O'Donohue, J. (1998). *Anam cara: A Celtic book of wisdom.* Harper Collins.

as a parting gift. A matching one hangs across from my desk at my home office still today. He cried as he read it and shared that we had been anam caras, or "soul friends." With this pronouncement, I cried, too. It was a profound honor to be considered Murney's soul friend.

Murney and I stayed in close contact until his death, speaking on the phone about every other week. When he became ill, my other close friend from Springfield, Brittany, called to tell me. I immediately took time off work to drive back to see him. He was in the hospital, nearing death. When I entered the room, he struggled to sit up as a great big smile stretched across his face, and he reached out to hug me. It reminds me of the smile when I first entered your hospital room, Dad. His death was the most profound loss that I had experienced at that time, and in ways it prepared me for your death.

My friendship with Murney opened me up to seeing friendship differently and helped me to become a better friend. Over the next several years, many of the close friendships I developed were with people much older than me. Maybe, in part, this was influenced by you being older—in your 40s—when I was born. For several years, I had significantly more close friends that were 20 or more years older than friends my age. While this has balanced out over time, most of my friendships are still older than I am, with many being 10, 20, or more years older. Even Heatherlyn is older than me, though that difference is negligible (and, as she reminds me, she still looks younger than me). I know that I am entering a period of life where I will be encountering a lot of grieving. This is a stage of life that most people face if they live long enough, but I am approaching it earlier than most.

About two years ago, I attended two Bruce Springsteen concerts. At both, he sang the song "Last Man Standing." In this song, he sings about the loss of friendships over the years. At the concert, he was on stage by himself with a spotlight just on him. Both times, I was overcome with emotion. One concert I attended with a friend who is a bit younger; the other I went to with a friend who is 10 years older. While I am not the youngest of my close friends and may not be the last one of us standing, the imagery of this song was powerful. I know I must prepare for the grief in front of me.

There is much struggle in this preparation. I do not regret developing so many friendships with people older than me. These have helped shape the person that I have become. I treasure and love these friends. It is good that I have also developed friendships with those closer in age and younger than I am. These will become important given the likelihood of the impending loss of other friendships. It is good that I have become good at grieving.

As these losses come, I know many will refresh my grieving of you. I will continue to love you and grieve you. This is the way that grieving often works. That's the deal.

Love,
Louis

With my mentor, Robert J. Murney

Letter 49
The Contingencies of Grieving

Dad,

It has now been just over a month since you died. A few people are still regularly checking in with me to see how I am doing. My answer varies and almost always includes, especially if it is someone new asking, that I recognize the grief will continue in different ways the rest of my life. My answer more commonly now includes pointing toward the struggle with the contingencies of grieving. So many things, by chance or symbolism, are connected in the grieving process. These contingencies have become the heaviest burden at this point of grieving. But maybe, they also hold the promise of opportunities that may emerge with the courage to face them directly. If I am honest, Dad, I am scared of some lessons that may emerge and their consequences. This type of fear is not common for me. Still, I face them.

Dad, I miss you awfully. Frequently, I wish that I could call and just have a short chat, even if in the state you were in during your latter days where you were not fully yourself. But there are so many other parts of losing one's father that right now weigh heavily and sometimes leave me feeling a little broken. It is harder to prepare for these given that many do not reveal themselves until I am amid the grief. While I have learned not to resist these, some embarrassment and even shame emerges at times with my response. I do not want people to think the contingencies are more difficult than the loss of you. As a therapist who has worked with grief, I often have witnessed clients struggling because of their resistance to acknowledging or facing aspects of the grief—these contingencies of grief.

Your death leaves many questions and unknowns, not the least of which is "What does it mean for who I am now that you are gone?" As I grew up, it was hard not to be known as Clarence Hoffman's son. This is often true in one's youth, especially in a small town like Charter Oak. But it is heightened when you are Clarence Hoffman's son, as it seemed you knew and were respected by almost everyone in the area.

There was one night that I had a bad basketball game. As usual, a group of us went to the one little restaurant in our town to meet up after the game. When leaving for home, I was still frustrated with the game, and those last few blocks up to our house I sped way too fast. Most mornings, I was the first to arrive at school to lift weights and shoot baskets in the gym. Coach Wiebers knew this, so that morning he was waiting at the door, leaning up against the vending machine as I walked in: "Had a rough game last night, huh, Lou?" After I acknowledged this, he revealed that someone called him to let them know that after 10 PM the previous night I was speeding up the hill to our home. While immediately embarrassed, there was also the recognition that if Coach knew you would know soon, too. The confession to you, Dad, started percolating within minutes of talking to Coach.

Even after leaving the small town, it was hard to shake the identity of being Clarence Hoffman's son. Much of this was that I internalized this identity and carried it with me. For years, I appreciated this. As I started to develop as a psychologist, this began to change, and my identity became more my own. But when going back to Iowa, the reality of being Clarence Hoffman's son outshined all that I had become. There is still meaning in being your son, but it is evolving now that you are gone.

This is one of many contingencies that I have been thrown into—some anticipated, some surprising. One that caught me off guard is the loneliness. Last weekend I flew home to spend time with Mom. John and Joy came a little before I left, too. When driving the rental car out of Denison, a deep loneliness settled in. It felt familiar in ways, like the loneliness I often felt when leaving Charter Oak growing up. Then, however, it was accompanied by a sense of freedom. The loneliness was different without it.

Your death brought a breadth of impact upon my relationships. Some have deepened while others have been challenged. More than anything, with my internal calling to return to the depths, the centeredness of who I am and want to be has changed the vantage from which I engage in all my relationships. Those who are similarly drawn to the depths feel closer; those who are afraid or averse to them have felt more distant.

Re-centered in the depths changes my view of many things—including myself. The pervasive question is, "How do I make sure not to dislodge from this place again?" It is not that my valuing or pursuit of the depths had been completely lost; nor was I completely disconnected from them. They were just not as present or centered in some aspects of my life.

There are lessons to be found in this space, including the loneliness that beckons more frequently than anticipated. And I have been drawn to, and even pursued, the loneliness at times when it emerged. My pursuit of these lessons has pulled me to my keyboard and to certain people in my life. Loneliness has not been a common experience for me over the past decade, and when it emerges it is almost always in the context of alienation within a relationship. It has become a guide helping me to understand relationships better. Some of the people I have been drawn to or not drawn to have surprised me, and some of these surprises have come with tears and pain. It is not only you that I am grieving.

Relationships often hurt. They wound and bless, and in the wake of grieving these realities were forced into view. Some relationships that I took for granted would be there for me at your death were strikingly empty, even wounding. Other relationships I never anticipated were very present in touching ways. Times of great need illuminate beyond what we may expect. The spotlight on the relationships in my life revealed what I could not have predicted. These contingencies have pushed their way to the fore of the grieving process, adding layers to the grieving while fortifying a new foundation. When we pursue a life rooted in love, often love strikes and blesses at the same time.

Dad, I hope you can understand this. Part of me resisted writing this letter, thinking that maybe this one would be better for my journal. I do not know if you would understand or maybe be hurt with my focus beyond you. Somehow there is a confidence inside me that you would understand.

Mom shared recently about how your own father's death impacted you. In her descriptions of your weeping and the depth of your pain, I felt both closer to you and a longing to have been able to experience such authentic vulnerability from you in the living years. In Mom's sharing, it was evident that this was the deepest heartbreak of your life. Her descriptions were of you crying in a way that I never saw you cry. You loved your father very much, but in Mom's sharing, I could also recognize how his death impacted you well beyond the grief. His death shaped how you engaged the world for years after he was gone—really, the rest of your life. You know the shattering that death or loss of a father can bring. I trust that you know the contingencies are not distractions, not looking away, not diminishing my grief at the loss of you. They reflect the power and space that you had in my life. Your being gone touches everything in my life.

With love and appreciation,
Louis

Letter 50
Forgiving

Dad,

There have been times when I resisted forgiving you. This was not out of stubbornness (though I can be stubborn!), resistance, or anger; it was an act of love and dedication. As a psychotherapist, I am aware that forgiveness is a difficult topic. While I recognize and appreciate the potential value of forgiveness, I often have seen it abused as part of a "flight to recovery" or a type of "spiritual by-passing."

As a flight to recovery, forgiveness may be proclaimed to signify that one is healed and no longer needs to do the difficult work of delving into one's relational pain and conflict. As spiritual by-passing, forgiveness is often regarded as a spiritual feat or act of faith that signifies a triumph. This may be pronounced to declare virtuousness. At other times, these may be the result of pressure from others to forgive.[1]

Then there are the popular cliches, such as forgiving not for the other person but to free oneself from the burden of anger and hurt. This, too, sounds nice; and sometimes it is authentic and works. However, these sometimes simplistic notions of forgiveness often are used in the service of suppression and later repression, which may contribute to complicating grief.

Forgiveness requires work, typically difficult work. Forgiveness is not something that is proclaimed; rather, it is experienced as part of a process. Frequently, forgiving is better attained indirectly. As one pursues understanding, empathy, and/or the repair of relational ruptures,[2] forgiveness emerges. In my own experience, which is consistent with what I have observed in clients and other relationships, attempts to forgive directly often encounter barriers or resistance, making forgiveness more elusive.

---

[1] These are examples that, in my experience, are common. They are not the only ways or reasons that one may engage in a flight to recovery or spiritual by-passing.

[2] There are times that encouraging understanding, empathy, relational repair, or forgiveness can be harmful, such as when one is still in a relationship with a perpetrator. Timing and context are important when considering when these are appropriate.

Dad, I did not pursue forgiving you in these letters, but I found it. I found it through deepening my understanding of you and our relationship. I found it through my empathy for struggles that you faced—and for your own humanity. I found it through recognizing your limitations. There are aspects of the forgiveness that may be partially based on my projections, some of which may not be accurate. Now that you are gone, I will never know. In some ways, it does not matter. I feel the empathy, understanding, and, most important, forgiveness in my body. There is a peace with it that I can relax into.

Every close relationship requires forgiveness. Relational depth generally cannot exist without it. There was not much at the time of your death that I felt the need to forgive, but what I did was important. And I am thankful for what emerged. It is part of what allowed me to feel closer to you through the grieving process. As these letters reveal, this was an earned forgiveness. I could not forgive without doing the work, and these letters allowed for me to do that.

Peacefully,
Louis

Letter 51
Being Broken and Happy

Dad,

In the last couple of weeks, I have found myself several times saying that I have become good at grieving. It is not easy; I have just become good at it. This does not mean that I look forward to grieving or move through my losses quickly. Rather, I found a way to dance and live in the presence of the losses. As bell hooks stated, "To be loving is to be open to grief, to be touched by sorrow, even sorrow that is unending."[1] Intuitively I knew that if I wanted to be good at love, I needed to be good at grief. And I deeply wanted to be good at loving with all my being.

The roots of this emerged in my Springfield years. I encountered the most difficult transitions of my life in these years, yet it was one of the happiest times of my life. The suffering was often intense. Lu Xun (2000) wrote, "When you put sugar into bitter tea, the amount of bitterness remains the same, it only tastes a little less bitter than without any sugar at all."[2] In Springfield, there was a lot of sugar in my tea, but I drank a lot of strong tea. I felt broken many times. I had a marriage that ended. I left the religious group in which I grew up. In the process of these transitions, I lost many—likely most—of my friends, including friends who became quite unkind.

Henri Nouwen wrote,

> Do not hesitate to love deeply. You might be afraid of the pain that deep love can cause. When those you love deeply reject you, leave you, or die, your heart will be broken. But that should not hold you back from loving deeply. The pain that comes from deep love makes your love ever more fruitful.[3]

---

[1] hooks, b. (2001). *All about love: New Visions,* p. 200–201. William Morrow.

[2] Lu Xun & Guangping, X. (2000). *Letters between two: Correspondence between Lu Xun and Xu Guanping* (B. S. McDougall, Trans.). Foreign Language Press.

[3] Nouwen, H. (1999). *The inner voice of love: A journey through anguish to freedom,* p. 51. Image.

Consistent with Nouwen, I have learned to dive into love. There is an unfathomable beauty and transcendent freedom in learning that loving deeply is worth being broken, even shattered. It is through being willing to suffer that I learned the power of relational depth, learned to love deeply. I will not be afraid of being broken on the other side of love. It was maybe the greatest lesson of my life. It freed me to not be afraid of the depths of love, even when knowing the relationship was temporary. In a worldly sense, all relationships are. This allowed me to savor not just the sunrise but also the sunset, with full knowledge of the impending darkness.

In my brokenness, I knew who I was and who I wanted to become for the first time. Prior to that, I had been seeking to become the person I thought that I should be. It was a suit with way too much starch that I was never meant to wear but hard to take off. It was my brokenness that allowed for this transformation, allowed for the growth. And I savored every tear that it brought. As I write this, I see how this prepared me for ideas to be encountered and ways of being that would shape my personal and professional life and values.

Through my friend Xuefu Wang, I was introduced to the Chinese term *zhi mian*. This term is not easily translated to English, but a rough approximation is "to face directly." The idea, however, is complex. It signifies facing oneself directly (an aspect of authenticity), facing others directly (similar to genuineness), and facing life directly (another aspect of authenticity). While in Springfield, I read a lot of Nietzsche and was drawn to and taught about similar ideas. One of my favorite quotes in these years was from Nietzsche, "All truths are bloody truths to me."[4] I was willing to earn my truths, sometimes with a brutality that was not kind to myself.

The possibilities connected to the brokenness I experienced bears similarities to Tom Greening's conception of existential shattering, which I have written about. My experience in Springfield was not quite the existential shattering that Tom spoke about, in particular because I sought it. In Springfield, I also listened a lot to the Indigo Girls, particularly the album "Become You."[5] This album contains many songs profoundly exploring life and relationships, including the song "Deconstruction."[6] This is what I was doing: deconstructing myself.

---

[4] As cited in May, R. (2004). On the origins and significance of the existential movement in psychology. In R. May, E. Angel, & H. Ellenberger (Eds.), *Existence*, pp. 3–36), p. 29. Rowman & Littlefield Publishers. (Original work published in 1958)

[5] Indigo Girls. (2002). *Become you* [Album]. Epic.

[6] Saliers, E. (2019). Deconstruction [Recorded by the Indigo Girls]. On *Become you*

Somehow, as I chipped away at myself, it never felt scary. I am sure this is, in part, because of the friends that surrounded me, especially Brittany, Murney, and AJ. But it was also because of an awareness that I was moving on to something new, something better. More important, it was authentic. The deeper, more genuine relationships were made possible by this greater authenticity, and the relationships helped me become more authentic, too.

In facing directly and engaging my brokenness, as well as other existential explorations, I began to recognize and, more importantly, embody the paradoxical reality that the joy and the tears were not separable. This is not a glorification of suffering. I do not seek or revel in suffering. Nor would I recommend this to others. But suffering is inevitable. There is no need to seek what will present itself to us in its own time; we just need to be ready.

In graduate school, I developed an interest in the study of theodicy, a philosophical endeavor to reconcile the reality of evil with an all-powerful and all-good God. I have since given up such pursuits. These seem to separate or justify suffering. This simplifies and distorts reality. Suffering exists and finds all of us, no matter how well we hide. Much suffering can never be justified. There is no justification or value in a child being abused, wars, racism, and genocide—all of which are occurring as I type these words. There is no greater good in the destruction of lives by earthquakes, hurricanes, and other disasters. These are tragedies, and any attempt to force meaning from their existence inevitably fails, often with the creation of more suffering. Yet, while these are devoid of inherent meaning or purpose, we can find or create meaning in the ashes. These ashes do not cleanse us or glorify us by their existence. But ashes can be used to nourish new life or create drawings of great beauty.

In Springfield, I learned not to be afraid to sit in the ashes. Or, as I have grown fond of saying, I have become good at sitting in the darkness and waiting for the light without the need to force the light to show itself. As a therapist, I view this as a powerful gift. It allows me to sit in places with clients that others are afraid to go.

Back in November, I took over much of your health care to help out Mom and John and started trying to call you most evenings. There was a lot going on in life in general, too. During this period, feeling overwhelmed with periods of stress and sadness was common. A few

[Album]. Epic.

nights during the winter that took the sun too soon even tempted me with periods of depression.

Over the last year, I realized this lesson again in a new way. Nathaniel Granger and I have spoken often about being happy despite life being difficult. The stresses and sorrows never became so great to allow no room for my happiness and joy. Dad, I am truly and deeply happy, and like you, I love life. Even these last three and a half weeks, when I have been seemingly continuously near tears, I have been happy. I have connected deeply with others and have loved and been loved. I am blessed. The brokenness will not take that away; nor will it take my centeredness.

Several of these letters have shared my experience and reflections on your optimism and our differences. Maybe this is my way of integrating an aspect of your optimism. It is a different path, and it leads to a different experience of optimism. While you sought to push out the darkness to let the light abound, I strove to have the dark and the light coexist in the same place.

Despite losing the lived reality of your love in my life, my experience since your death is of more and deeper love. In part, this is the love shown to me by those who care about me, but it is more than that. bell hooks, in *All About Love*, wrote, "Confronting the possibility of dying I became obsessed with the meaning of love in my life and in contemporary culture."[7] While not my own death, the confrontation with your death, building on the momentum of lessons from many losses over the past several years, has provoked reflections on love and suffering. As I have discussed, I developed the conviction that I would not allow fear of loss or being hurt prevent me from loving deeply. Learning this at the embodied level, not just as an intellectual assertion, was one of the most profound lessons of my life. Now, I love; it is who I am.

I am not perfect at loving. There are the times that I have fallen away from living and embodying the depth of love that I desire to live by. Your death has revitalized this conviction—this embodied conviction. I do not want to stray from it again. There is much loss in my future, but with each loss there is a deeper, growing conviction that the knowledge of future pain will not prevent me from loving deeply. The pain can be withstood, but I am not willing to live without the depth of courageous love. In this love, there is deep joy that overshadows the impending pain.

---

[7] hooks, b. (2001). *All about love: New visions*. William Morrow.

At an earlier time in my life, I would have felt pangs of guilt for being happy right now. Happiness would have seemed to dishonor you. I bought into the lie of appropriate emotions for a situation. The years wading in existential waters (and existential literature) has freed me from this deception. As a psychotherapist, I have helped clients understand and experience something beyond this deception, too.

So tonight, I hurt. I still cannot fathom a world without you, and I miss you terribly. But I am blessed.

Your blessed son,
Louis

Letter 52
Your Hands, Part II

Dad,

This is the final letter of the book, but I hope not the final letter. I hope that I will keep writing these letters for years to come. It could be a way of staying connected to you—still conversing, even if one directional. I hope very much for this.

As I contemplate this final letter, I return to thinking about uncomfortable chairs, chasing the monsters away, and your hands. In the last months, I spent my time in uncomfortable chairs at your bedside. I sat in them in the hospital, then in the nursing home, and then back in the hospital those final days. At times, this was hard. After the first visit, where I spent most of a week at the hospital, my back hurt for several days. But it was worth it. I imagine, too, that there were nights, and days after, when your back hurt from sitting in the old brown chair late into the evening and sometimes morning hours.

I do not know how well I succeeded in chasing any monsters away. Most of the time I am confident I was successful, especially on some of the phone calls when you were confused and angry at Mom. The monsters faded and you were able to sleep. There was a brown chair in the hospital room, too. It was darker and more comfortable than the chair in my room growing up. But it seemed fitting that in your room that last night there was an uncomfortable brown chair. And it seemed fitting that I sat in that chair, at times holding your hand, chasing the monsters away.

I want to remember that night. It was a painful night. I watched so many times you grimace in pain. I watched as the confusion became more prominent and any clarity further away. I did not know if you knew it was my hand holding and stroking yours. Likely, you thought it was Mom's hand. I thought about this in that brown chair and came to the conclusion that it did not matter. All that mattered is that you seemed to experience some comfort. When you grimaced, stroking your hand helped. When you looked up confused, holding your hand seemed to assure you. I am familiar with the research on the power of oxytocin to help with pain and anxiety. If my words could not comfort maybe my hands could—even if a little.

The best memories do not always have to be happy memories. Sometimes, they can be painful memories infused with meaning. The memories from that night were not joyous, but they were beautiful. Holding your hands, I sometimes felt more connected to you than I had in a few years. And often during those years, I longed for that connection. I found bits and pieces of it, but as you slipped away, there were fewer of these moments and not as deep as that night.

Tears fill my eyes once again as I type the final words of this letter because I long to stay connected with those last moments of holding your hand and chasing the monsters away. It was such a beautiful sorrow and connection.

I love you, Dad. I am still grieving, and I am thankful that I will still be grieving for years to come—for the rest of my life. It is a grief that I will treasure and hold in love. You were a father worth missing.

Love,
Louis

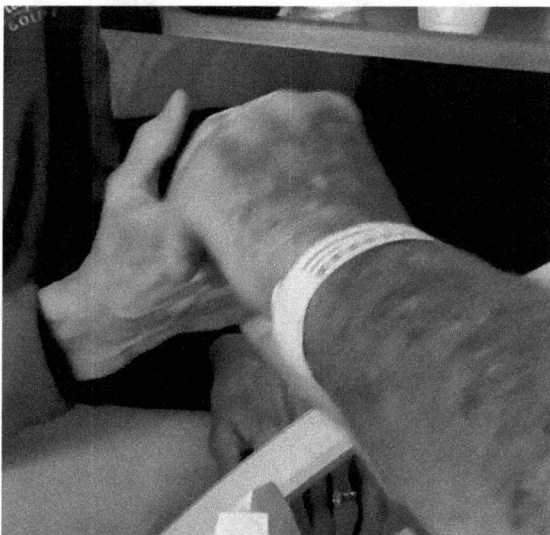

My parents holding hands a few hours before my father's death

Closing Reflections

Writing this book has broken me and opened me up. It exposed wounds and allowed me to work toward healing them. It has helped me face pains that I was avoiding and reclaim aspects of myself I had lost. It has broken my heart and cradled my heart. It has exposed my isolation and deepened my love for my father while deepening connection with many beloved people in my life. It has exposed weaknesses and limitations in myself and in my relationships while leading me to greater relational sustenance. These are the perils and gifts of facing grief and oneself directly. I am thankful for it all and better for the grief and suffering. While I wish my father was still here, my life is more vibrant after engaging this process than it has been in some years. I am still crying more; however, I am also feeling the joys of life more deeply. These are lessons I had learned intellectually and emotionally before, even experientially a few times, and lessons I have taught for years. But they are more palpably present in my life thanks to *Letters for My Father.* If no one reads the book, it still has transformed me.

When I first started sharing early drafts of this book, I was both excited and afraid. I had come to believe that this book had something valuable to offer, but I feared maybe this was all self-deception or self-aggrandizement. Waiting for the feedback was difficult. The first words of feedback came from my good friend, Xochitl, after she read the first few chapters and texted that she was "already crying." Soon Nathaniel, my closest and most trusted friend, offered affirmation. Then my mentor, Myrtle Heery, shared her endorsement. My mother then my brother Mike shared their encouragement. It remained hard to believe, and I feared that it was just their connection with me. This feedback from some of the most important people in my life helped me begin to believe that this book maybe could impact and help others. The most encouraging of these affirmations was when people revealed shedding tears and saying that my love for my father came through.

In a conversation with Nathaniel as he nearly finished reading the manuscript, he said there was a beauty in brokenness. This has been a sentiment that I have lived by for years and explored in a chapter he had not yet reached. Some of the greatest beauty I have witnessed in my life are faces of people I love and care about strewn with authentic tears. It is not the suffering that is beautiful, but rather the openness to suffer—to trust that there is something beautiful that can result in directly facing life and suffering. The trust, honesty, and vulnerability enhance and deepen this beauty. Any walls or barriers I have in the presence of these tears quickly melts away. Often, without touch, I have felt the embrace as if a hug from across the room when seeing these tears trace down someone's face. These tears never grow old or lose their power.

When we are broken, there are aspects of ourselves hidden in our day-to-day life that are revealed. Even the most self-aware person will at times be surprised by what they find when the blows of life expose us to ourselves. Grief with the interplay of loss and facing mortality can reveal precious aspects of who we are. A few of the lessons in this book I desperately wanted to resist and deny, but the draw to learn from them and allow them to transform me had a stronger pull. While many onlookers may not recognize the change, the early months following my father's death have been profoundly transformative.

My relational landscape looks quite different than it did a few months ago. Some relationships have stepped up while others stepped back. As I write this closing about a month after the rest of the book was finished, the tears for my father are less frequent while tears connected with other relationships and the contingencies of the grieving process are more present. In the midst of this, my life is very full of love. I am more centered, whole, and committed to being the person I want to be.

Part of me does not want this book to be done. I want to keep exploring, reflecting, and learning—and I want to continue grieving and loving. There is a fear that the renewed connection with my father could fade when I no longer return every few days to tinker with a letter or two. But I know it is time. Even writing these words brings a sense of sadness.

If you have stayed with this book to the end, thank you. While I wrote earlier in the book that what I benefited from it was achieved in the writing, there is meaning to be found in my grieving process and helping others with their own life. When Nathaniel told me yesterday that he was feeling more emotional and connected with other people's sadness and grief as he finished reading the book, it became apparent that it was time to free the book so that hopefully it may bless the life of others.

Epilogue

In the introduction and then again in several of my brother's final letters to Dad, Louis shared that he has become "good at grieving." I clearly remember when Louis first spoke those words to me. It was several weeks after Dad had passed away. Louie and I, along with Mike and Michelle, had spaced out our visits to Mom. But because of complex schedules, there was a short overlap between Louis's visit and mine. In a few moments over coffee and breakfast, Louis said, "John, I'm pretty good at grieving." It seemed like an odd statement because most folks, including those who are good at grieving, do not think of grieving as something one becomes good at doing. To test my sense that his statement was peculiar, I searched the Internet later that afternoon for "I am good at grieving" using a few different browsers, but I only found a handful of search results. (By comparison, I found hundreds for "I am good at making mistakes.")

My brother *is* good at grieving, and I am glad he was willing to share his letters in this book, perhaps as a guide to those of us who are not so good at grieving. Part of what makes the letters special is the fact that not only is Louis good at grieving, he is also highly skilled at helping others to grieve. He has learned how to help people navigate some of the most difficult parts of their grief journeys in ways that are healthy and meaningful.

As for me and my journey, I had already experienced intense moments of grief during Dad's final years, and especially his final months, but there was still important grief work for me to do. During these last months, hospitals, dementia, limited mobility, and nursing homes converged to unleash demons Dad had held at bay for most of his life. Dad was a strong man, and he likely prayed that he could take his demons with him to the grave instead of having to confront or them, or worse, to reveal them to others. Dad would rather suffer intensely alone than share the battle with others. Part of this was an effort to shield the people he loved from pain, but as Louis articulated well through his letters, part of this was also to keep others from knowing the demons existed at all. The irony is that we might have loved him even more deeply had he shared those demons.

After receiving the doctor's call, my wife Joy and I got back to Iowa about 12 hours before my brothers. Michelle and Mom were there, and we witnessed Dad in terrible agony during his final morning. I was overwhelmed with grief and pain. I knew the importance of Dad consciously seeing Louie and Mike one more time, so I asked the nurse to hold off a while with the next-level pain medications until they arrived. I am grateful that Dad was able to recognize Louie and Mike when they arrived and to have moments of touch and connection before he faded from consciousness into peace.

For weeks after Dad died, I was unable to explore my grief beyond the sense of relief that he would never again battle internal demons or experience agony like he did that final morning. I am the president of a regional public university and also a two-year technical college in Northern Minnesota, and these are challenging times in higher education. I am fortunate and grateful to have an amazing cabinet of truly exceptional humans. Dad was particularly skilled at hiring great people, and I would like to think I have tapped into some of his legacy in this regard. When the doctor's call came, I left without a moment's hesitation, and my team ran the university and college without me for the next two weeks. When I returned, I was not at my best and I made some uncharacteristic mistakes, but my team was forgiving.

I recall one challenging moment in particular. I would like to think I do a pretty good job of being emotionally available and present as a president. I was in an intense meeting, and a faculty member expressed how difficult decisions I had made affected her personally. One of the burdens of leadership is that there are times when the best we can do is choose among flawed options. I had learned from my father not to hide behind the reality that the decisions were the least harmful among the options available. Instead, I leaned into her experience and apologized. It did not matter to this faculty member that other decisions would have been worse for our institutions, students, and community. What mattered to her was her own experience and the experiences of colleagues whom she cared about deeply. The decisions were mine, and they resulted in harm, so I apologized. As I spoke the words, a sincere tear came to my eye reflecting the authenticity of the moment. But then the moment changed. I felt a surge, and it took everything I had not to cave into a barrage of my own tears. For me to cry in that moment would have shifted the energy away from this faculty member in her time of need and back to me. Later, when I returned to my office, I tried to let go and cry, but the moment had passed. By damming up my emotions, I could no longer access the tears I knew I needed to shed.

The job demands remained substantial through the following weeks, and I did not create space to grieve. I confessed to my team that I was not 100% and asked for their forgiveness and their help. We had gone through some very difficult times together, and I trusted them as more than just employees or colleagues. They are also friends. Their love and care for me was sincere, and I was able to access a few tears with them, but I had built up a strong dam to hold back the flood of tears in other moments. A well-built dam is not easy to tear down.

When I returned to Iowa, I only had a few hours of overlap with Louis. I wanted to be there for him, and I am grateful to read in his letter to me that he found meaning in our time together. Mostly, however, he was there for me. Perhaps Louis found meaning in the moment because he was able to quickly and gently guide me toward the first steps for tearing down the dam that was separating me from my grief. Louie understood that I was not only saying goodbye to Dad; I was also wrestling with deeper meaning I had associated with Dad and our relationship. It was one thing to miss Clarence Hoffman, but it was another to wrestle through all that he represents to me about life, relationships, leadership, parenting, vocation, community, and more.

A few weeks after Louis and I had connected, Chrissy Downwind, Vice President for American Indian Student Success at Bemidji State and Northwest Tech, asked me to join her and her brother, Michael from White Earth, for a private smudging ceremony. I had talked with Chrissy about my conversation with Louis, so she knew I was progressing into deeper aspects of grieving. During the ceremony, the smoke of the tobacco seemed to free my heart, mind, and spirit. Chrissy and her brother talked about grief, and I found myself wrestling with some of my brother's words about losing what Dad meant to me. Suddenly, I experienced Dad's hesitation in transitioning from life on earth to life beyond. I experienced his fear about reconnecting with his father, who had died several months before I was born. Our family had talked about Dad reconnecting with brothers and friends or drinking a beer while sitting on a lanai with Cliff, my father-in-law, whom Dad loved and who had passed away 13 years earlier. But it had never occurred to me to think of Dad reconnecting with his father. I said something about this to Chrissy and her brother, and they mused that Dad's father might have fought his way through the crowd of people anxious to welcome Clarence so that he could be the first to embrace him. My tears became full of life, and the next words from my colleagues faded as I took in more tobacco smoke and spoke with Louis in my mind. He was there reminding me that just as our father feared he had disappointed his dad, we feared disappointing our dad. As I journeyed, grief asked me to do something more than let go. It beckoned me to embrace and open myself up to receive the embrace of others.

This is just a small part of my story with Louis—how he is good at grieving, and how he is good at helping others to grieve. When Louis got into the car to drive home from the funeral and the ideas began to come to him, he could easily have shaken them off and focused on the drive ahead. That is likely what Dad would have done. Instead, Louis listened. He asked his oldest son for help: "Can you drive us home?" And by asking for help, he created space to start writing these letters, which has been an important part of his journey with grief for our father. Perhaps that is one of the great lessons of this book—at least it is for me.

John L. Hoffman
June 19, 2025

Lessons from Letters for My Father
Olivia Michael & Edbury Enegren

Reading Louis's letters to his father, loved ones, and others centered around his grief after his father's death inspired us to gather lessons about grief. In the same way that grief is different for every person and relationship, the experience of witnessing grief will also vary from person to person and depends on their unique relationship with the griever, as well as their personal grieving experiences.

With that said, we offer two unique perspectives on grief, along with takeaways or lessons about grief that might resonate with you, the reader, and perhaps inspire you to reflect on your own unique ways of grieving and being.

Olivia's Perspective

Letting Go of Idealization Allows for a Deeper Love
Idealizing a person takes away from the chance to love more deeply. It is freeing to give yourself permission to fully experience people—the good, the bad, and all that is in-between. Many times, this creates a pathway for greater self-acceptance of the good, bad, and in-between within us. It is hard to grieve an idealized version of our loved ones. It can surely feel disappointing and painful to realize the person you have put on a pedestal is flawed; however, breaking that perfect idea you have had about your loved one can allow you to have a deeper and more meaningful relationship with them, even after they are gone. Also, letting go of the idealized version of your loved one can help you to accept your own imperfections, allowing you to build a stronger relationship with yourself and your values.

Vulnerability Creates Connection
Leaning on people can be difficult, but grief often invites us to lean on our support system, even when it feels uncomfortable. Being vulnerable, leaning on your people, and asking for help creates an opportunity for the people in your life to show their love for you. It is good to be open to this, but hard if you are someone who highly values

your independence and fears burdening others. Even when hard, it can be valuable and worth the courage to allow oneself to enter into vulnerability.

Pain and Regret are Part of a Life that is Fully Lived

While pain and regret are difficult feelings to experience, they do not necessarily mean that you have done something wrong. They indicate that you have lived freely, made difficult decisions, and loved deeply. Imagine what kind of life someone must live not to have any regrets or guilt—perhaps a very restricted life. There is a lot of beauty that can be found when you directly and imperfectly face life and love.

Pain is a Teacher, but Not for a Reason

When someone is grieving or suffering, a common and often unhelpful response they receive is that "everything happens for a reason." This can feel quite disempowering and frustrating to a person navigating the depths of grief. While often this is said with good intention, it falls flat. There is no reason that justifies pain and suffering. Pain does not need a reason to exist. What is more meaningful is exploring how suffering shapes us. How it forces us to stretch and grow, understand ourselves more fully, and clarify our values. This is not a process that can be rushed or forced upon a person who is grieving or suffering. However, with the passage of time it can allow you to reflect on ways your pain and grief has changed you. Speaking from my own experiences, I have endured darkness and suffering in many ways. After living through those difficult experiences, I was able to notice how they changed me. I was forced to grow and stretch in ways I may not have been able to without the suffering. I was able to understand myself in new ways and strengthen my values. In the midst of my suffering, the sentiment "everything happens for a reason" would not have been well received. There is no justification for some of the suffering I experienced, but as time passed, I gave myself permission to acknowledge and even appreciate the ways that pain and suffering have helped me become the person I am today.

Grief is a Mirror and a Guide

Loss has a way of revealing what matters most. Grief allows you the opportunity to reflect on things that you want in your life, things you hope to change, conversations you do not want to miss, and so much more. Though sometimes in a harsh way, grief connects us to ourselves more deeply, connects us to the person that we loved and lost, and helps us identify what we value most as we continue to live our lives.

Grief is Ongoing and Ever-Changing

Believing that grief will have an end date can be a huge disservice to your grieving process. Grief may never end. However, it will continue to change shape. Grief can ebb and flow like a tide, and it is okay to lean in and out of its depth. Some days may feel light as you fondly remember fun or sweet memories of your loved one. Other days may feel very heavy as you struggle to imagine going on with your life without the physical presence of your loved one. It can feel freeing to give yourself permission to go where grief takes you, at times allowing it to wash over you. It is natural to wonder when the pain will subside. While there is no timeline for this, it can be helpful to remember that the prolonged pain you feel can serve as a reminder of how deeply you loved and still love a person—and even keep you connected to them. The thing about grief, though, is that it can be so complicated. It will look different for every person and relationship. It is valuable to allow yourself to grieve in the way that is organic for you. There is no wrong way to feel when navigating grief.

Grief is a Living Relationship

While the death of a loved one often feels like the closing of a chapter, grief is a living relationship. Your loved one lives on in your life through your grieving and remembering. The letters in this book are a part of the relationship between a grieving son and his late father. They represent something alive, not dead. They are a medium to express and process regret, grief of lost time and lost opportunity, and an immortal love. Writing letters are one way to keep your relationship with your lost one alive, but there are endless ways to do this. When navigating grief, it is worthwhile to explore how you can keep your relationship with your lost one alive and active if that is something you long for.

Edbury's Perspective

When Louis asked me to contribute to this book, I felt honored. I also felt uncertain. I have only known him for two years. How could I add anything meaningful to such an intimate work? But as I read through these letters, I discovered that witnessing someone else's grief can teach us as much about ourselves as about the person grieving.

Grief Creates its Own Landscape

In Letter 43, Louis writes about "living in a space that no one else can inhabit." This line stopped me. We talk about grief as if it follows predictable patterns. As if there is a right way to do it. But Louis's letters show something different. Each loss is its own world. This individuality extends beyond just the differences in grieving from person to person. It varies from loss to loss within the same person. Louis's grief for his father was not what he anticipated it would be. It differed from his grief for Amaya, from his grief for friends and mentors he has lost.

The rituals that comfort us in one instance may feel hollow in another. The emotions we expect may never arrive, while others we never imagined possible may overwhelm us. Even the lessons we identify here likely will not, and need not, apply to many people or instances of grief. If grief followed a universal process, it would not be personal to the specific relationship. That uniqueness also connects us.

Let Grief Surprise You

At the outset, Louis notes that if he had known the path his grieving would take, it would not have been as effective. This stayed with me through the whole book. When we try to anticipate or control our grieving, we close ourselves off from what it might teach us. Grief refuses to be planned. It brings unexpected gifts alongside its pain.

While reading these letters, I was continually struck by the emotions Louis discovered—not just sadness, but profound joy in memories, anger at unresolved conflicts, guilt and the value of what it teaches, even happiness amid tears. By remaining curious about his grief rather than trying to control it, Louis allowed these surprises to transform him. This curiosity is part of what Louis means when he talks about facing grief directly.

Loss Shows Us What We Carry

Throughout the letters, Louis engages in remarkable self-reflection. The loss of his father became a new lens through which he examined his life: his career choices, his parenting, his struggles with touch and vulnerability. These insights might have been possible without the loss of his father, but grief made them urgent and immediate.

Louis discovered patterns he had carried from his father, both those he cherished and those he struggled against. He recognized how his father's difficulty with conflict had shaped his own avoidance patterns. He saw how lying on the hard floor beside his son's bed connected him to his father sitting in that brown chair years earlier. These discoveries are not just intellectual. They change how Louis sees himself, how we see him.

Connection Outlasts Presence

One of the most profound lessons from these letters is that death does not end connection. In Letter 11, Louis writes about preserving his father in himself through grief, giving "meaning and purpose that transforms the suffering." Throughout the book, he describes moments of feeling closer to his father after death than during the living years.

This is not about denial or refusing to accept loss. Louis fully acknowledges what has ended—the possibility of certain conversations, the physical presence, the shared future. But he also discovers what continues: the internalized voice, the preserved memories, the ongoing influence. Through writing these letters, he created new conversations with his father, finding answers in the process of asking questions.

Grief Asks Us to Hold Contradictions

Both Louis and his brother John mention that Louis has become "good at grieving." In the short time I have known Louis, I have also heard this said by and about him. But what does it mean to be good at grief? While some letters address this directly, the collection itself stands as a possible path to grieving well. Being good at grieving does not mean avoiding pain or moving through it quickly. It means being able to hold multiple truths simultaneously. It means to be broken and happy, to feel profound loss while remaining open to joy.

We see this again and again in the letters. He can sob while listening to father–son songs during a bike ride with his son. He can recognize the imperfections in his relationship with his father while still treasuring their love. Maybe being "good at grieving" means learning to live with these contradictions instead of trying to fix them.

Witnessing Grief Changes Us

As I read through these letters, something unexpected happened. I felt envious of the depth of Louis's grief. I am not proud of this. My own father died when I was young, and we were already estranged. Would any loss in my life generate such profound reflection? This envy made me feel distant from the text—distanced from Louis—alienated by its intensity.

But as I continued reading, Louis's vulnerability began working on me. His reflections on mentoring made me examine my own relationship with him as my supervisor and teacher. His struggles with accepting help reminded me of my own difficulties with saying no to opportunities, including this one. His insights into his father revealed Louis to me in new ways, just as his grief surfaced aspects of his father for him.

By the book's end, I found myself recognizing something essential: the isolation inherent in grief. When Louis writes about inhabiting a space no one else can enter, he is naming a fundamental truth. His mother, his brother, everyone who loved Clarence Hoffman experiences their own unique grief. No matter how public the mourning, each person ultimately faces their loss alone.

This recognition dissolved my earlier envy. Instead of feeling alienated by Louis's depth of feeling, I felt connected through this shared human condition. We all face losses. We all struggle to articulate what those losses mean. Hopefully, we all discover that grief transforms us in ways we never anticipated. The landscape differs, but the territory is one we all must eventually traverse.

Reading this book reminded me that witnessing grief can also be its own profound experience. We do not just observe someone else's pain; we are changed by it. Their vulnerability invites our own. Their insights prompt our self-reflection.

This is why Louis chose to share these letters. Not because he had answers about how to grieve correctly, but because sharing the experience of grief is generative. In reading about his journey, we are invited to examine our own losses, our own relationships, our own willingness to face life directly.

The lessons I have drawn from these letters feel both deeply personal and broadly applicable. They have made me think differently about my own losses and the losses yet to come. They have challenged me to consider what it might mean to grieve well.

About the Contributors

Olivia Michael, MA, is daughter, sister, aunt, friend, and lover of life. Professionally, she is a third- year clinical psychology PsyD student and works as a psychotherapist at the Center for Humanistic and Interpersonal Psychotherapy, a subsidiary of the Rocky Mountain Humanistic Counseling and Psychological Association. Olivia has had a supervisory and mentorship relationship with Louis for just under one year.

Edbury R. Enegren is a second-year doctoral student in clinical psychology at the University of Denver, where he also works as a psychotherapist. Over the past two years, he has been privileged to learn from Louis Hoffman as a student, supervisee, and mentee. When not sitting with clients or contemplating mortality, he can be found in the company of his cat, his garden, or the friends who have become his chosen family.

Other Books on Grief
By Louis Hoffman

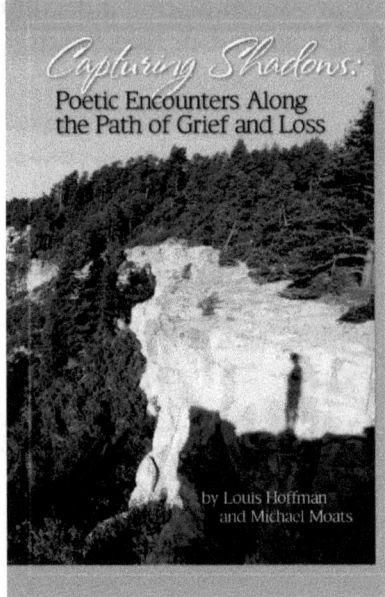

Capturing Shadows:
Poetic Encounters Along
the Path of Grief and Loss

by Louis Hoffman
and Michael Moats

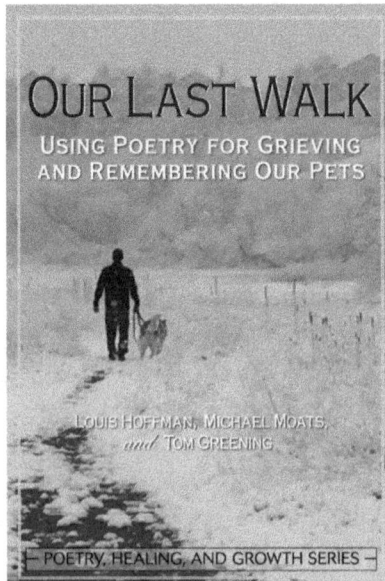

OUR LAST WALK
USING POETRY FOR GRIEVING
AND REMEMBERING OUR PETS

LOUIS HOFFMAN, MICHAEL MOATS,
and TOM GREENING

⊢ POETRY, HEALING, AND GROWTH SERIES ⊣

About the Author

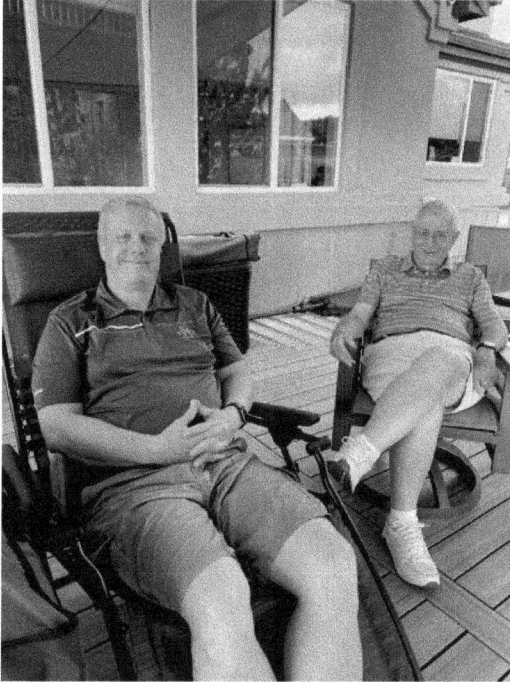

Louis Hoffman, PhD, is a son, husband, father, friend, and dog companion. Professionally, he is a licensed psychologist, the executive director of the Rocky Mountain Humanistic Counseling and Psychological Association, and the Editor of *The Humanistic Psychologist*. An avid writer, he has written or edited over 25 books and over 100 journal articles and book chapters. Due to his contributions to professional psychology, he received the 2020/2021 Rollo May Award and has been named a Fellow of the American Psychological Association and seven of its divisions (1, 10, 12, 32, 36, 48, 52). Dr. Hoffman teaches and provides clinical supervision at the University of Denver and is a supervisor at the Center for Humanistic and Interpersonal Psychotherapy. He maintains a private practice in Colorado Springs. During his free time, he enjoys reading, writing, hiking, close time with friends, and bicycle riding. For more information about Dr. Hoffman, visit https://www.louis-hoffman.com.

Dr. Hoffman's other books on grieving and loss include *Capturing Shadows: Poetic Encounters Along the Path of Grieving and Loss* (with Michael Moats) and *Our Last Walk: Using Poetry for Grieving and Remembering Our Pets* (with Michael Moats and Tom Greening).

What does it mean to lose a father? A deeply personal, moving account of one man's relationship with his dad, through the lenses of grief, love, and forgiveness. In a series of letters, the book journeys through key contemporary issues including racism, masculinity, and the meaning of success. Dr. Hoffman describes his process of accepting his father as he was and bringing the humanism that defines all his relationships into the heart of his relationship with his father. An honest and insightful exposition of loss, vulnerability, and the yearning for relational depth. We need to love our broken, hurt world and to heal it through a life of kindness and compassion.

Mick Cooper, PhD, Professor of Counselling Psychology,
University of Roehampton, London

In his own moving words in *Letters for My Father,* Louis Hoffman models a "healthy, honest grieving process." A father–son relationship is precious beyond words, yet Louis has, through his deep love for his father and their relationship, found the right words to move the reader and himself through grief with smiles and tears. Louis's authenticity as a son shines a brilliant light on the grieving process of losing a father. In my over forty years in a psychology career, I have had the great honor of listening to Hospice Bereavement groups and writing about grief. I know these letters will be insightful to those living through the grieving process. I highly recommend this book to everyone, especially fathers and sons.

Myrtle Heery, PhD,
Author of *Awakening to Aging* and *Tracking Kindness*

Before I made it through a handful of letters, I was weeping. I cried many times as I proceeded. My tears were not only for the depth of love and grief in the letters but also for the courage beckoning from the pages. The words were an invitation to dip into the human experience of love and grief. The words asked me to sit with the complicated ways in which humans relate, and how having the courage to show up is more than half the battle. As my own father(s) grow older and I recognize their time is running low, this offering of love reminds me to not waste any time, to be sure to take the time to say all the things that need to be said. Love is easy; relating is harder. Relating requires bravery, vulnerability, authenticity, a willingness to let others sit with us in our brokenness, trusting that they will hold us, and accepting that maybe

One part touching tribute and one-part personal processing, Louis Hoffman's candid and probing *Letters for My Father* captures a son's devotion to a towering and loving, if ultimately imperfect, figure in his life. At the same time, it offers an intimate and sustained gaze at the deep themes in their braided lives, bravely and vulnerably laid bare for the reader. Far from self-indulgent, Hoffman pivots deftly from reminiscence to reflection in letter after letter, seeking the emotional truth of a father–son bond and its wider relational ripples in an outpouring of letters to, for, and about his father, and the mirror that his living and dying held up to them both. For anyone who is drawn to correspondence with the deceased as a therapeutic tool for authentic grieving, I say, "Read this book." And to any who doubt the capacity of grief to add existential depth to our fragile existence, I say, "Enter into an imaginal conversation with this author."

Robert A. Neimeyer, PhD, Director, Portland Institute for Loss and Transition, and Author, *Living Beyond Loss: Questions and Answers about Death and Bereavement*

In this collection of 52 love/grief letters, each one a gem in its own right, Louis Hoffman allows the reader to share in his highly nuanced and profoundly authentic reflections on and (re)constructions of his continuing multi-faceted loving relationship with his deceased father, situated within a unique historical, political, cultural, and personal wider web of bonds and meanings. Hoffman can draw on a wealth of experience and insight as a psychologist, therapist, and scholar, and I felt touched by how true he is to his humanistic and existential heart, speaking with the very personal voice of a son. His ponderings on both individual life and universal existence come not from a distanced height but from the depths of the lived life, being radically present to process and to what it means to be human. As a psychologist, therapist, and grief and bereavement researcher, I found this book to be a deeply moving and insightful contribution to the literature and recommend it to practitioners and bereaved clients alike. As a daughter whose father died nearly a year ago, I found that the book inspired me to enter into fresh conversations and more courageous (self)-reflections of my own.

Edith Steffen, PsychD
Editor, *The Handbook of Grief Therapies* & *Continuing Bonds in Bereavement*

inspires resilience and strength in those whose lives he touches. I can't help but feel that his father would and did recognize that from a very deep place. What is remembered, lives! He has ensured his father's immortality through these letters he has written, as well as through his own ongoing work in the world. Dr. Hoffman consistently stands up for integrity, truth, and authenticity in times when they are sorely needed. Thank you, Dr. Hoffman, on behalf of us all who feel distinctly witnessed in our own soul loss and recovery in grief, as we yearn and strive to transform pain into beauty.

Drake Spaeth, PsyD
Director, Existential-Humanistic Psychology Specialization,
Saybrook University;
Past President (2019-2020),
Society for Humanistic Psychology (APA Division 32)

What a rare gem this book is! Louis Hoffman shares with us his unconditional love and wisdom for his departed father in very compelling and intimate language. The book made me feel that I had met both these men in these pages in a rare and profound way through the journey of reading it. I especially love that this book was written with the fierce urgency of "daimonic" wisdom that Louis transparently and humbly shares with us. His process is simultaneously very raw and yet also sophisticated. All sorts of rich paradoxes emerge spontaneously in the letters that he writes to his father with also simple but powerful truths. His central concern is a genuine and open-ended concern to find the truths emerging in his heuristic-like exploration of his grief. However, Louis withholds very little about his process and journey and openly discusses many of the most important issues about life itself in this book. He seems auspiciously free of any attempt to steer the flow of the current of his emerging awareness and wisdom to arrive at some predetermined conclusion or even towards a conclusion at all. A very helpful book for all of us and also a real gem of humanistic wisdom for anyone fortunate enough to read these words.

Ian Wickramaskera II
Faculty, Fielding University

In *Letters to My Father*, Louis Hoffman writes honest and vulnerable letters that explore the complexity of grief after the death of his father. The letters provide insight and encouragement for others finding their they won't but we will be okay anyway. Parenting, and being parented, is a life-giving, soul-shattering, expansive experience that can bring us the heights of joy and the depths of despair. This book offers readers the opportunity to experience both.

L. Xochitl Vallejos, PhD, Editor, Lullabies & Confessions
Board Chair, Rocky Mountain Humanistic Counseling &
Psychological Association

The Irish say when your father dies, you lose your umbrella against bad weather. Thrown this circumstance in his life, for Louis Hoffman it was like having to become that umbrella for his father. His deeply personal account of this journey, boldly recorded here, invites us all to face our own essentially lifelong struggles, our longing for closeness and need for differentiation, our memories both painful and healing, our hopes both dashed and realized, our guilt and our grief, and more. Rich in precious ephemera, the warmth of a smile, the touch of a hand, the tear on a cheek, may these pages draw you into a more truthful and profound understanding of what it is to be human and to be a self.

Erik Craig, EdD
Psychologist, Independence Scholar, and Author
Past President, International Association for the Study of Dreams
Past President, Society for Humanistic Psychology

Even as there is no one or correct way to grieve, as Dr. Hoffman says in his wonderful book *Letters for My Father,* the reader will find a candid, poignantly vulnerable, and exquisitely insightful reflection on grief and the journey of bereavement that gifts a rich validation to anyone living with the loss of a significant loved one. Not since C. S. Lewis's *A Grief Observed* have I encountered such a sublime gateway to one of the most difficult and loving experiences we will ever have as human beings. More than anything, Dr. Hoffman shows that even as we experience grief and loss as something that diminishes us, leaving an unfillable vacuum in our soul, it can also be the ultimate culmination of love—the thing that illuminates us in the fullness and richness of our humanity! Dr. Hoffman embraces this paradox with grace, humility, and courage. It is clear to me that he embodies and carries forward the best of his father's qualities and legacy in his own unique way. Aware that he is not an optimist like his father was, he places a high value on facing life directly with courage and honesty—and he does so in a way that reverberate across generations. Yet here, the author demonstrates how reflective grief can become a generative act. For clinicians, *Letters for My Father* provides valuable insights into individuation and mourning in the adult father–son relationship. For any reader, it is a brave and beautiful testament to love made stronger through loss.

H. Luis Vargas, PhD, LMFT
Private Supervision Practice
Founding Director of Clinical Training,
Center for Humanistic and Interpersonal Psychotherapy

I have known Dr. Louis Hoffman as a friend and colleague for the past two decades. We have collaborated on a few book projects and this is the book that felt most intimate because of the courage of vulnerability evident throughout. In addition to providing plenty of wisdom as to how an existential approach can impact one's grieving, the sharing of Dr. Hoffman's heart space inspired me to open up my own heart space to myself and others. I know the book will do the same for you.

Mark Yang, PhD
Author, *Lighting the Candle: Taoist Principles in Supervision Conducted from an Existential-Humanistic Perspective* and *Existential Psychology and the Way of the Tao*

In the lost art of letter writing, Louis invites the reader to accompany him through an intimate path of a son's grief. Seeking to humanize, rather than create a false idolization of his father, he openly pours his heart out to his father about his reflections on the love, struggles, gifts, and regrets within their relationship of father and son, as well as how a new lens of introspection was birthed through pain. As grieving is different with each person and each loss, Louis offers an opportunity to share in his approach of actively engaging grief through the written word.

Michael Moats, PsyD, psychologist and author of *Sunrise Through the Darkness: A Survivor's Account of Learning to Live Again Beyond 9/11* way through grief. Oftentimes, there is unresolved conflict and a need for honest conversation after the death of a loved one. This book shares a therapeutic process for grief and self-exploration. Dr. Hoffman illustrates how writing can be a powerful tool for self-exploration and emotional healing. His letters guide readers through the tangled emotions that grief stirs, revealing how growth and clarity can emerge when we give voice to our pain, contradictions, and hopes. Personally, I was profoundly touched by the honesty and exploration of family relationships within *Letters to My Father*. Dr. Hoffman's letter writing brings us to the universal wisdom that joy and sorrow coexist. The letters demonstrate that relationships do not end with death; we continue to be transformed. In this book, the process of letter writing offers readers a process to cultivate continuing bonds, understanding, and growth after the death of loved ones.

Terri Goslin-Jones, PhD, Faculty, Saybrook University,
Author of *Life's Concerto:*
Wholeness through Poetry and Expressive Arts

Beauty in brokenness. Paradoxes of grief. *Letters for My Father: Grief, Love, and Self-Exploration* is truly a tour de force, depicting, as its name implies, the lived experience of grieving the loss of a father. Hoffman's letters explore the depths of love, the paradox of emptiness and fulfillment, and the beauty in brokenness that can sometimes only be experienced posthumously. Louis, I am extremely grateful and palpably humbled at the invite into your grief—your world—your soul.

Nathaniel Granger, Jr., PsyD, Past President,
Society for Humanistic Psychology
Editor, University Professors Press

Letters for My Father offers a moving and mature reflection on the father–son relationship, skillfully weaving a narrative that honors the complexity of familial love. Written through the eyes of a son in mourning, these letters capture not only personal grief but also a developmental journey through the later phases of the family life cycle—where adult children re-evaluate their parents with both compassion and clarity. The emotional tension present in these pages is never gratuitous; rather, it reflects a courageous commitment to truth-telling that respects the enduring bond between parent and child. In family systems theory, we understand that unresolved conflict can